Book of Coffee

ANNE VANTAL is a freelance journalist. She has collaborated on several books on subjects as varied as the cinema, the English countryside and renewable energy sources. She is the author of the *Les Grands Moments du Salon de l'auto*, published by Éditions E.P.A. in 1998.

First published by Editions du Chêne, an imprint of Hachette-Livre
43 Quai de Grenelle, Paris 75905, Cedex 15, France
Under the title *Le Café*
© 1999, Editions du Chêne – Hachette Livre
All rights reserved

Language translation produced by Book Production Consultants plc, Cambridge

This edition published by Hachette Illustrated UK, Octopus Publishing Group Ltd.,
2–4 Heron Quays, London E14 4JP
English Translation © 2004, Octopus Publishing Group Ltd., London

Printed in Singapore by Tien Wah Press
ISBN 13: 978-1-84430-117-1
ISBN 10: 1-84430-117-6

Anne Vantal

Book of Coffee

HACHETTE
Illustrated

Contents

GUATEMALA
AEREO   Q.0.05

Woman drinking coffee. Poster by Henri Meunier for Rajah coffees, Belgium, 1897.
Paris, Library of Decorative Arts.

Introduction

There is something mysterious about coffee. Just ask a group of children how it is made, and nine out of ten will tell you that they have no idea, unless they imagine a cereal reduced to powder...

There is something magical about coffee. The dregs can be used to read the future! And that blackness – a colour rarely found in our normal diet – conjures up memories of witchcraft, of the time when coffee seemed to have come straight from Hell.

There is something commonplace about coffee. It is a faithful support at the start of our day and when we are tired. But who pays it any real attention?

There is something exotic about coffee. Unlike its cousin, chocolate, however, it does not usually make our mouths water in anticipation. And if we know anything about its distant origins, it is thanks to the advertisements that capture the rhythms of Cuban salsa, Brazilian samba or African drums.

There is something paradoxical about coffee. It is familiar, yet unknown; sophisticated, yet banal. We love it without knowing anything about it.

Yet.coffee is the result of patient and demanding work. Twenty million people all over the world participate every day in the great coffee chain. Coffee requires loving care at every stage in its life, its final quality depending as much on the painstaking labour on the plantations as the scrupulous monitoring of its transformation.

Even the most meticulous cultivation and accomplished roasting, however, are never enough, on their own, to make a good coffee – thumbing its nose at all scientific laws, coffee is above all a matter of pleasure. And, in the realms of pleasure, we can all write our own laws.

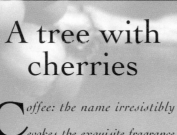

A tree with cherries

Coffee: *the name irresistibly evokes the exquisite fragrance of freshly roasted beans. Before it reaches our cups, however, coffee is nothing more than the seed of a tropical shrub (with many varieties) that will only bloom through sun and shade, heat and rain, loving care and.... plenty of patience.*

Classifying coffee

Everybody is familiar with the two kinds of coffee available on the market: Arabica and Robusta. This apparent simplicity, however, obscures a complex web of classifications with subtle distinctions that are lost on the uninitiated.

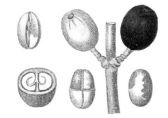

Below
From the seed to the plant: germination takes place after eight weeks.

The slender stem resembles a matchstick until the first pair of leaves appear.

A LATINISM
Botanical classification requires every plant to be defined in terms of its family, genus, species and variety. In the 18th century, when the French botanist Antoine de Jussieu (1686–1758) set about classifying the coffee trees he had just encountered, he was at first convinced that they displayed the characteristics of jasmine and for a while gave them the name *Jasminum Arabicanum*. A further, more detailed study led him to put the coffee plant into the family of the *Rubiaceae*, which also includes the madder, cinchona and gardenia. He went on to invent the genus *Coffea*, a Latin neologism based on the noun "caffé" (the French term for coffee at that time). The Swede, Carl Linnaeus, who had been studying the cocoa tree, turned his attention to coffee in the 1750s.

Above
The botanist Carl Linnaeus described thousands of plants, including coffee. Print by Bertonnier, 1833.

ARABICA, CANEPHORA

Two species of *Coffea* are found in nature: *Coffea Arabica*, which grows in the wild on the plateaus of Ethiopia, and *Coffea Canephora*, found in the forests of tropical Africa. The former goes by the generic term "Arabica coffee", whereas the latter is mainly known for its most widespread African variety, the Robusta, which has given its name, by extension, to several of the types of *Coffea Canephora* grown today. Many varieties of *Canephora*, however, have beans that are at best tasteless and at worst unappetising, and so are of no interest to coffee drinkers.

Above
The flowers of a coffee tree cluster round the base of the leaves. *Coffee from Arabia*, print by Coignet, after Bessa. 19th century. Library of Decorative Arts, Paris.

Top
The coffee tree is a shrub with a gangling appearance and slightly droopy branches

Opposite page, below
Fruit and bean (detail).

Coffees by the dozen

The varieties of Arabica distinguished by coffee producers include Typica, Bourbon, Pointed Bourbon, Mocha and Marella, as well as hybrids like Mundo Novo and mutants such as Moragogype, which first appeared in Brazil. The Robusta, native to Africa, is the most widespread variety of *Canephora*, although other, less common crops, often incorrectly termed Robustas, can be found, such as the Kouillou in Madagascar and the Niaouli in Togo and Benin.

Jasmine or sloe?

Once a coffee tree has matured, it flowers exuberantly two or three times a year. Coffee plantations exude a heady fragrance that once suggested a kinship with jasmine.

AN EVERGREEN BUSH

Left to its own devices, the coffee tree grows upright, easily attaining heights of five to six metres – or even more in the case of a Robusta – but on plantations it is pruned to more modest dimensions. It is usually propagated by cuttings, but it is also possible to sow seeds reserved from the

previous harvest, although this method has the disadvantage of losing some of the characteristics of the mother plant. The young plant is lovingly pampered in a greenhouse before being transplanted outdoors, where it can live up to fifty or sixty years, thirty of these in full production. The tree first sprouts its main branches, which it is incapable of renewing (and which are therefore never pruned), and then some secondary ones, which must be ramified as the tree grows older. The foliage is persistent and the tree never loses its leaves.

Above and right
The white flowers with five or six petals bloom in groups of about ten. Their highly fragrant blossom lasts only a few hours.

Background
Coffee tree, print by Laplante after a drawing by Faguet, taken from the *History of plants* by Figuier.

Opposite, below
Postcard with a botanical illustration of Arabica coffee.

Cohabitation

The tropical climates that suit coffee trees often play havoc with the rhythm of the seasons: periods of rain alternate with dry spells and the temperatures stay more or less constant. This is why the coffee tree can flower several times in the same year. As a result it can occasionally have flowers and fruit of varying degrees of ripeness side by side on a single branch, in the same way as some citrus trees. This may be delightful to look at and smell, but it does not make harvesting any easier.

INTOXICATING FRAGRANCES

Two or three times a year, if it rains heavily after a period of relative dryness, a coffee tree adorns itself with magnificent white blossoms in corollas. Their strong fragrance recalls that of jasmine or the orange tree or – according to the Danish writer Karen Blixen, once the owner of a coffee plantation in Kenya – the wild sloe. The coffee tree only starts flowering in its fourth year of life, but after that it can produce twenty to thirty thousand flowers a year. This fairy-tale whiteness is short-lived, however – once they have ensured pollination, a few hours after blooming, the flowers no longer serve any purpose. They wither very quickly to allow more time for the fruit to form.

"*Coffea Arabica L.*"
0,50
CORREIO BRASIL 74
CASA DA MOEDA DO BRASIL
Bicentenário da Cidade de Campinas

The philately of coffee

What can be more delicate than miniature images of a sprig of coffee in bloom or red and green cherries on the same branch? For many years now the coffee-growing countries have been aware of the aesthetic possibilities of their crop.

From the coffee branch...

Philately traditionally finds excellent sources of inspiration in local plants and animals. The coffee tree is no exception to this rule, as it offers striking vignettes with beautiful contrasts of reds, whites and greens and delicate filigrees of its ephemeral blossoms.

Early on in their philatelic history, major coffee producers like Colombia and Brazil understood the mysterious fascination that the plant exerted on their eventual consumers overseas, and so they often reserved the pictures of coffee trees for their airmail stamps.

...to the industrial world

Philately has not forgotten that coffee is a basic product

Cerises de café 10F
RÉPUBLIQUE DE CÔTE D'IVOIRE
Cycle du café
BAILLAIS
POSTES

Coffea arabica
VENDA
COFFEE INDUSTRY

GUATEMALA AEREO Q.0.12
TALLER NAC. — GRABADOS EN ACERO—GUATEMALA

Far right
Guatemala – which produces superb varieties of coffee, such as Antigua –

has issued a series of stamps depicting the entire chain of production for coffee.

2/6
KENYA UHURU 1963
COFFEE INDUSTRY

that plays a key role in trading relationships, and the current trend is to diversify stamps by evoking not only coffee flowers or fruits but also the whole chain of production, from bean to cup. The results have been equally delightful, although there is one

50 FILS YEMEN ARAB REPUBLIC
2 RIALS YEMEN ARAB REPUBLIC

Left
Coffee branches illustrating stamps from Yemen.

Above
Harvesting scene on the high plateaus of Kenya

shortcoming: the recipient of a letter cannot enjoy the subtle fragrance of either a coffee tree in bloom or freshly roasted beans.

Recently, stamps have tackled the theme of work on coffee plantations: picking Robusta in Cameroon, or harvesting and drying in Venda (South Africa).

Cherries and beans

Botanists may use the technical term "drupe", but the fruit of the coffee tree is more generally known by the nickname "cherry". It does indeed resemble a succulent cherry, but inside it contains not one stone but a pair of beans.

Below
The fruit of the coffee tree, commonly called a cherry, turns red as it ripens.

Right
Coffee beans are extracted from the cherries; their size and colour varies according to the species: small and greyish in Robusta, longer and bluish-green in the Arabicas.

A WELL-PROTECTED TREASURE
When the flowers fall off the fruits start to form – a process that takes up to six or seven months. Once it is ripe, the fruit greatly resembles a cherry: the same round or ovoid shape, the same size and the same colour, gradually turning from green to yellow, then to orange and finally to red. The skin surrounds a thick, viscous pulp. Inside that, a husk – pale yellow in colour but known as the silver skin – protects the two green coffee beans – each marked by a long, deep furrow – nestling in the heart of the fruit; these are tucked together with their convex sides facing outwards and their flat sides facing each other.

FROM SMALL SEEDS…
Every species of coffee tree produces its own beans, which differ in size and colour. Some varieties are considered more generous than others, and producers take great pains to increase their yields. The annual production of a coffee tree does not exceed three kilograms of cherries, which amounts to five or six hundred grams of beans.

Once these beans have had their silver skin removed and been dried and roasted, they will serve to make around forty cups of the precious nectar...
If all the threats to the life of a coffee plant are taken into account, this statistic offers plenty of food for thought!

Below

Cherries that are still green can co-exist on the same branch with others that are completely ripe. Hand picking on on an individual basis is therefore the only way to secure a harvest of uniformly ripe cherries.

The height of some coffee trees (here in Java) requires the use of a ladder.

One of a kind

It can happen that a cherry contains just one bean, instead of two. This single bean, rounder than the norm, answers to the melodious name of "caracoli", reputedly derived from the Spanish word *caracol*, meaning "snail". The Germans prefer to call it a "coffee pearl". A much sought-after rarity, caracolis are assiduously sought out by some coffee merchants and sold separately to especially demanding customers. In some quarters they are considered to have a concentration of aromas beyond compare; for others they are merely a biological curiosity, with no distinctive taste. The caracoli is usually found in the last cherry on a branch, right at the tip. In some species of Arabicas, however – for example, those of Costa Rica – up to 30% of their yield usually comprises caracolis, with productivity restricted as a result. This goes a long way in explaining the exorbitant price of the caracoli bean.

Under the volcano

The coffee tree, with its fragile health, is famously difficult to grow. It has exacting requirements with respect to climate, soil, sunshine and rain. These are all determining factors that help give each type of coffee an inimitable flavour.

BRACING MOUNTAIN AIR

Coffee was born in Africa but has gradually spread to other continents along the belt between the two tropics. The coffee tree is vulnerable to the cold, so these latitudes provide it with the climate that it needs: temperatures of around 20° C all the year round, heavy rainfall and a substantial environmental humidity. The Robusta is, as its name suggests, more... robust, and it can endure greater variations in temperature. Nevertheless, all coffee trees require not only at least 1,200 to 1,500 millilitres of rain per year, evenly spread out over the course of the months, but also a location sheltered from strong winds. The Arabica has an extremely good head for heights, as these guarantee it a degree of coolness, and it leaves the stifling mugginess of the great tropical plains to its less finicky cousin. It is impossible to find Arabica below heights of 600 metres.

Background
Coffee plantation in Brazil, early 19th century.

Engraving by Salathe after Steinmann.

Above
The Colombian coffee trees planted on high mountain slopes benefit from the natural shade of cloud cover on the peaks.

Opposite
The deep and fertile volcanic soil of Central America is ideally suited to the roots of the coffee tree.
.

Furthermore, it has no fear of mountain peaks, and in Central America it is not unusual to find coffee plants at altitudes of up to 2,000 metres above sea level. In fact, the higher it is planted, the better the coffee, as the fruit takes longer to ripen when the heat is less intense. This element of time is significant in building up a greater concentration of tastes and aromas.

OUT OF THE SUN, INTO THE SOIL

Although the coffee tree loves the sun, it shuns its direct rays and prefers to stay in the shade. In the wild it rears its head up into the clouds – on steep escarpments shrouded in sea mists -– or nestles under the giant trees of the African forest. Coffee trees also require fertile soils rich in humus. The leaves that fall on the ground by a coffee tree are usually left undisturbed, as they serve to enrich the soil. It is best suited to soils that are "acid" – lacking in limestone – and sufficiently deep to accommodate roots that sometimes extend for over a metre. It is therefore not surprising that the best Arabicas have made their way to the slopes of large volcanoes, because they thrive on the altitude and argilo-silicious soils and find the climatic conditions ideal. Such sweeping generalisations do not tell the whole story, however: in reality, any soil that supports coffee also contributes a little something of its own, just as land leaves its mark on a wine – and importers who select beans once they leave the plantations pride themselves on being able to use their senses to detect the origins of each and every one.

Above
The state of Karnataka in South-East India is acclaimed for both its Robustas and Arabicas. In Asia the blossoming is guaranteed by the arrival of the monsoon.

Below
Coffee plantation in the valley of the River Ozosi in Costa Rica. This country comes tenth in the world ranking of coffee producers, with 150,000 tonnes of coffee per year.

The peregrinations
of a bean

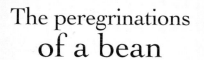

Coffee, born somewhere near the
Red Sea, took centuries to
complete its trip round the world.
Assiduously coveted by the powers that
be, the coffee tree became a symbol of
the wealth of the Arabian caliphs and
the great colonial empires, as well as a
witness to the suffering of thousands
of Africans who were snatched from
their homes and reduced to slavery.

The goatherd and the dervishes

Once upon a time there was a little goatherd... The history of coffee, like so many others, starts with a legend. It has been reworked and retold by Arab story storytellers down the ages.

Below
Wandering dervish in Turkey
Print by Folkema,

18th century. Religious devotees were responsible for spreading coffee throughout the Arab world.

THE LEGEND OF THE GOATHERD

Once upon a time, somewhere in Yemen, there lived a goatherd called Kaldi. He grew exasperated by his animals as they never seemed to get tired and were so noisy and frisky at nights that they prevented him from sleeping. Exhausted, he went to the village's wise men, who set about studying the behaviour of the goats. They noticed that the animals gorged themselves on wild berries growing on the hillside. Intrigued, they tried out these amazing fruits for themselves and soon felt reinvigorated. They had fortuitously discovered the effects of caffeine.

THE COFFEE OF THE DERVISHES

This Arab legend, which is retold in *The Thousand and One Nights*, overlooks the fact that the coffee plant was originally native not to Yemen but to the high plains of Abyssinia (now Ethiopia). It also failed to mention the date on which this great discovery was made. We do know, however, that the Persian doctor and philosopher Avicenna (980–1037) recommended coffee as a cure for certain intestinal disorders in his *Canon of Medicine*, and that the nomads of Abyssinia had a centuries' old tradition of drinking an infusion of crushed green coffee beans.

Above
The great sage Ibn Sina, also known as Avicenna, investigated the benefits of coffee and promoted its consumption.

The roasting of coffee was probably also discovered by chance, after coffee trees burnt in a bush fire gave off a delectable fragrance. What is certain is that this practice was developed by Muslim dervishes keen to fulfil their duties of night-time prayers, as they recognised that this plant had the power to keep them awake. On their annual pilgrimage to Mecca, they introduced coffee to their fellow pilgrims throughout the Islamic world. Before that, however, the plant had already crossed the Red Sea – undoubtedly also via religious networks – and the shores of what is now Yemen were studded with coffee trees. By the mid-15th century, coffee was established in both Persia and Arabia.

Double-page spread
Joseph Vernet, *Entrance to the*

port of Marseilles. Paris, Louvre Museum.

Left
Coffee harvest in the Portuguese Indies
According to legend, Baba Budan, an Indian Muslim from Mysore, introduced coffee growing to the Malabar Coast when he brought back some beans from his pilgrimage to Mecca.

Below
Al-Razi, a 9th-century Arab physician, described some of the properties of coffee.

The right stuff?

Although coffee was introduced into Muslim customs by devout men who took it as a stimulant for their religious observances, it has not always found favour with the authorities in Mecca. There was even talk of making it comparable to alcohol and forbidding it altogether but, when the authorities debated the issue, they were unable to come to an agreement. The holy scriptures of Islam gave no formal indications on the matter, so a compromise was reached: the drinking of coffee was advised against, but this did not prevent anybody from drinking it.

The wine of Arabia

From being the secret of mystic brotherhoods and isolated doctors and botanists, coffee went on gradually to conquer the entire Orient. In 1453 the fall of Constantinople to the Turks soon brought this nectar into the hands of merchants in Marseilles and Venice.

THE MERCHANTS OF MOCHA

The banks of the Red Sea are home to a city with a magical name: Mocha (or Moka). Founded by a Sufi mystic who had travelled in Africa, this oasis was for many years little more than a modest hamlet. The port grew rich through trading in spices, which were coveted by merchants pouring in from all over the Orient. By the mid-16th century it had grown into a thriving city that welcomed ships bound for destinations as far-flung as

The Ibled company sings the praises of its coffee. This firm, founded in 1824, specialised in chocolate and other "exotic" produce.

Istanbul, Cairo, Aleppo and Damascus. When the coffee tree was introduced to the high plains of Mocha's hinterlands, the green beans were transported to the coast on the backs of camels or mules, and Mocha became the world's foremost supplier of coffee. Anxious to protect their riches, the Arab rulers monitored all the sacks before their departure. Not a single green coffee bean set to sea without having been scalded beforehand, thus ensuring that no seeds could escape in a state of germination. Abyssinia and, above all, Yemen, were then the only producing countries – and would remain so until the mid-17th century –

Above
Poster for Moka-Maltine, by Dudley Meath, c. 1900. Paris, Library of Decorative Arts.

moka

Bunn and qahwa

The word coffee was long thought to be derived from its place of origin, Lake Kaffa, in Ethiopia, but this theory overlooks the fact that the local language, Amharic, refers to it as *bunn*.

The obscure origins of this word are more likely to be found in Arabic, Turkish or Persian. There is, however, no doubt that the terms *moka* and *qahwa* were in common parlance in the Muslim world by the 15th century. Moreover, this Arab word *qahwa* resembles all the other designations of coffee, from the Turkish *cahve* to the English *coffee*, from the Italian *caffè* to the French *café* (which for a long time was written as *caffè*, as proved by the article Diderot devoted to it in his Encyclopaedia, first published in 1765), or the hybrid *caoua*, an imitation of the Arab word that was popular among French colonialists in North Africa.

BUNN

caoua

and the sultans sought to preserve a lasting monopoly over a trade that guaranteed their prosperity.

EUROPE ENTERS THE COFFEE TRADE
The great discoveries and spirit of adventure of the Renaissance suddenly broadened horizons and, before long, the West began to hear about the existence of coffee through the reports of Mediterranean merchants who had sampled the "wine of Arabia". In the early 17th century Venice imported its first coffee, purchased in Cairo. There followed an intensification of both commercial and diplomatic contacts, resulting in a flourishing spice trade. Then the Europeans decided to eliminate the middlemen from the Levant and fetch coffee themselves from the ports of the Red Sea.

Above
Audience granted by the Sultan Mahmud I to a Venetian ambassador, in Constantinople, around 1740. 18th-century, châteaux of Versailles and Trianon.

Background
The port of Mocha in Yemen, in the 19th century Print by Blondeau, after Fleury.

caffe

COFFEE

qahwa

Europe discovers coffee

Although the English could boast about being the first Europeans to enter the port of Mocha, future events would show that it was the Dutch who really sealed the fate of this Yemeni town.

Right
Young woman drinking coffee, a 17th-century Dutch painting. The Dutch were among the first Europeans to drink coffee.

Below
Man of quality drinking coffee pub. by F. G. Jollain, 1688.

DUTCH PILFERAGE

In 1600 Queen Elizabeth I granted permission for the creation of the East India Company, an independent firm that would not come under the control of the British crown until 1874.

The Dutch fully understood the significance of this unprecedented financial venture and were quick to form their own East Indies Company. In 1616 a ship from the Dutch company put in at the port of Mocha to load up with green coffee. The captain also took advantage of an opportunity to steal a few cherries; he took them straight back to Amsterdam, where the seeds were planted in the greenhouses of the Botanical Garden. Nobody could have guessed the fabulous future that was in store for them.

PAPAL BLESSING

The 17th century marked the highpoint of Mocha's glory. In 1663 the Dutch started to trade directly with Yemen. In 1664 the Frenchman Jean de La Roque brought some sacks of coffee to Marseilles after a long journey in the Orient and invited a select few to whet their curiosity by tasting it. The port had to wait another forty years, however, before it received its first imports of coffee. The dark colour of this beverage so beloved by Muslims aroused the suspicion

Coffee from Sri Lanka

In 1658, the former Portuguese possession of Ceylon (now Sri Lanka) was occupied by the Dutch, who substantially increased the cultivation of spices and introduced coffee. In 1796, the British seized several towns, and in 1802 they colonised the whole island. Ceylon went on to supply the entire Empire with coffee, which had been greatly appreciated in London ever since the 17th century. In 1869, however, all the Ceylonese plantations were devastated by a veritable plague of rust, caused by a fungus. The British authorities' only solution was to replace coffee with another crop: tea. Thus it came about that the good citizens of the Empire learned to drink this new beverage and took to it with all the passion for which they have become famous.

of Christians, who believed that it was the sign of a diabolical blackness. The Pope was asked for his opinion; as soon as he sampled the drink he was won over by its charms and immediately issued a timely authorisation. Reassured, the apothecaries of Marseilles started to sell coffee, and the pharmacists in Lyons followed suit, although the strange nectar had still failed to win over Paris – and the King.

Below
Tea and coffee, print by J. T. Grandville for

The lively flowers, 1843. Paris, Library of Decorative Arts.

Top
Joseph Vernet, *Interior of the port of Marseilles*. Paris, Naval Museum. Marseilles was the first French city to discover coffee.

The fad for things Turkish

Suleyman Aga's visit to Paris prompted French aristocrats to ape Oriental customs. They sported turbans and brocaded tunics, greeted each other with elaborate bows and peppered their conversations with exotic terms.

In 1770 this trend became a target for Molière's scathing wit in *The Bourgeois Gentleman*, whose protagonist was overly eager to welcome a mysterious Turkish "Mamamouchi" in quest of his daughter's hand. This play was extremely popular, and cleverly demonstrated that bowing and scraping were not the same as gentle breeding and manners.

Top
In the 17th century the Turkish ambassador, Suleyman Aga, earned his place in the history of coffee by making it fashionable in France.

THE AMBASSADOR OF THE SUBLIME DRINK

Coffee made its first appearance in the Court of Louis XIV in 1669 with the arrival of the Turkish ambassador, Suleyman Aga, sent to France by Sultan Mehmet IV. He received noble Parisians in a fairy-tale Oriental setting of unprecedented luxury and served the drink typical of his country. It was considered too bitter, and somebody had the idea of adding sugar to it. After that, it was a sure-fire success. Only the Sun King – perhaps irritated by the ways of his somewhat gaudy visitor – spurned coffee in favour of yet another novelty: chocolate.

BATAVIAN SUPREMACY

Europeans refused to tolerate the Arabs' tyrannical control over coffee and set out to conquer new territories in Asia and the New World, with the aim of establishing their own plantations. In the 1750s the Dutch, who had succeeded in germinating their coffee seeds in Amsterdam, shipped some Arabica shoots to India and Ceylon and then, forty years later, planted some coffee trees in their new colony of Batavia (on the island know known as Java).

Batavian coffee sounded the knell of Arab prosperity and propelled Holland into the top ranks of coffee production.

SOME USEFUL PRESENTS

Paradoxically, it was the city of Amsterdam that gave France its first coffee trees in 1713, after the signing of a peace treaty. Louis XIV had them replanted in the 17th century King's Garden in Paris. Two years later, the Sultan of Yemen, making the best of unpropitious circumstances, thanked the French king for a service rendered by sending him several dozen coffee sprouts. All that remained was for them to find a home.

Left, below
Jean-Baptiste-André Gautier-Dagoty, *Madame du Barry being given a cup of coffee by Zamor in her dressing room*, 1771. Versailles. The Court of Louis XV was partial to coffee, and the King reputedly roasted his beans himself. His favourites, Mesdames du Barry and Pompadour, were equally enthusiastic.

Right
Young Turkish girl drinking coffee, 1707–1708. Paris, Library of Decorative Arts.

The tenacious chevalier

The first coffee trees planted on Caribbean soil – in the French Antilles, in the early 18th century -– were only able to fulfil their historic destiny thanks to the tenacity of a French infantry captain.

THE FRUIT OF PERSISTENCE

Gabriel de Clieu, a young lieutenant from Dieppe, was promoted to the rank of infantry captain at the age of twenty-three. Louis XIV gave him a post in Martinique, where he settled and, in 1718, gained the title of chevalier. Captivated by his adopted home, de Clieu dreamed of making improvements and planting new crops. Having learnt that the King's Garden in Paris had some precious coffee plants, he made repeated requests and finally achieved a royal authorisation, with the help of de Chirac, the King's doctor. In 1720 Louis XV – who by now had succeeded his grand-father to the throne – entrusted the chevalier with two young plants, so that he could try to acclimatise them to the Caribbean.

A DANGEROUS CROSSING

On 8 October of that year de Clieu left Rochefort onboard the *Dromadaire*, with two cuttings sheltered from the cold by glass-covered frames that spent the nights in the captain's cabin for greater safety. The crossing was not without incident: after an

Above
The chevalier Gabriel de Clieu. After 20 years in Martinique, he moved to Guadeloupe, being appointed Governor there in 1737.

Right
De Clieu on the voyage to the New World, sharing his water ration with one of the coffee plants that he hoped to acclimatise to Martinique.

Left
Coffee harvest in Martinique, 1853.

attack by pirates – fortunately swiftly resolved – a ferocious storm obliged the crew to dump ballast: reluctantly, they parted with their surplus fresh water. The subsequent lull did not bring an end to their mishaps. Deprived of wind, the *Dromadaire* was becalmed in the sea off the Antilles, only a short distance from its destination. The sailors were afraid of dying of thirst in the muggy heat and the coffee trees, which had grown during the voyage, were also feeling the strain. Faithful to his promise to the King to look after the plants more than himself, de Clieu shared his meagre water ration with them. When he finally arrived in Saint-Pierre, the chevalier disembarked with the one sole coffee plant that had survived the journey.

THE START OF A LINEAGE

Gabriel de Clieu planted the coffee tree in his own garden, where it became an object of great desire until, some eighteen months after its arrival, it yielded a kilo of cherries which the chevalier freely distributed. Soon afterwards, fruits were also taken to Guadeloupe, and then to Santo Domingo; the era of coffee cultivation in the Caribbean had begun.

Left
The Arabica coffee plant, botanical plate by G. Regnault, in *Botany within reach of all*, 1774.

Conquering the world

Holland's plantations in Asia dominated the coffee market until the beginning of the 18th century, when France took the lead with her Caribbean exports, which began in 1736. This triggered a race in which other European nations sought their share of the market. Meanwhile, the craze for this new beverage was sweeping through Paris and beyond.

THE LANDS OF THE NEW WORLD

In the course of a single century the coffee-growing lands came to cover the entire tropical belt in both hemispheres. From Martinique, the beans gradually spread to the entire Caribbean. In 1730 the British planted some cuttings in Jamaica, unaware that they would later produce one of the finest coffees in the world. Haiti, Cuba and Central America also joined the club. Meanwhile, in 1715, the Dutch had cannily sent some coffee plants to Surinam, their possession in Guyana. Just as in Mocha a hundred years earlier, a thief managed to poach a few cuttings – but this time the victim was Dutch and the robber was French, and French Guyana became a coffee producer in its turn. History repeated itself, as the French then lost some plants to the pilferage of the Portuguese, who were clearing land in Brazil. Paradoxically, Colombia, now second in the league of coffee producers, had to wait fifty years for

Top
The produce of the French colonies: coffee from the Comoro Islands.

Left and right, below
Grinding coffee on a plantation in Surinam, in 1858. Details.

The Dutch were pitilessly implacable with their slaves, and rebellions occurred on a regular basis.

the chance to grow coffee, at the instigation of Spanish priests.

COFFEES FROM FURTHER AFIELD

Like its neighbours, France was anxious to expand its coffee production and so explored new possibilities. Louis XV, who greatly appreciated the new drink, asked the botanist Antoine de Jussieu, who was studying coffee in Paris, to send some specimens by boat to the new garden of Pamplemousses, on the northern coast of the Île de France (now Mauritius).

Above
P. de Rosemond, *Coffee growing in the Île Bourbon* (now La Réunion). Paris, National Museum of the Arts of Africa and Oceania. Encouraged by the French East Indies Company founded by Colbert, coffee thrived on the island. At the start of the following century it was replaced by sugar cane, which was considered more profitable.

Perfidious beauty

In 1727 the Portuguese realised that Brazil was the perfect environment in which to cultivate coffee – but, unfortunately, they had neither plants nor seeds. The government of Parà, which is now Belem, in the north-east of the country, there-fore found a pretext to send Palheta, a young officer, to French Guyana on a simple mission: to ask the Governor, M. d'Orvilliers, for a few cuttings. In the event of a refusal, he was to steal some.

M. d'Orvilliers had his orders from the King and handed nothing over. His wife, however, was unable to resist the charms of the young lieutenant and, when he was about to leave, she slipped a few coffee cherries into his hand. Thus it was that Brazil, now the world's greatest coffee producer, owes a piece of its history to the treachery of a beautiful Frenchwoman.

Left
Coffee plantation in Brazil in the early 19th century. Print by Salathe.

Below
Flying bridge for the embarkation of coffee in the island of La Réunion Anonymous, c. 1730–1740.

From Mauritius, the coffee trees moved on to the neighbouring island of La Réunion, then called Île Bourbon. The plants, which all came from a particularly variety, were dubbed Bourbon coffee, and they are still grown under that name today, albeit in regions very remote from the Indian Ocean.

A century later a new type of coffee tree, the *Canephora Robusta*, was found in the great forests of Africa, and it proved considerably less delicate than the Arabicas that had been grown until then. The Dutch were the first to take advantage of this discovery: they were soon obliged to substitute Robusta for all their Arabica plants in Java, as these had been devastated by rust.

Above
Rakoto,
*Picking coffee in
Madagascar*.

Paris, National
Museum of the
Arts of Africa and
Oceania.

"ME ALSO FREE"

Coffee and slavery

Coffee, said Michelet, "nourished the adult age of the century, the great age of the Encyclopaedia". The minds of the philosophers, stimulated by the beverage, would perhaps have displayed less vivacity, however, if not for the forced labour of thousands of slaves. The 18th century may have been the Age of the Enlightenment, but it was also the century of slavery.

A triangular commerce

The Dutch were the first to establish a colonial administration based on the forced labour of their local subjects, and their commercial rivals were not slow to follow suit. However, the growing demand for coffee in the 18th century "obliged" the major powers to resort to the slave trade on a large scale. By 1730 slaves from Africa were arriving in Haiti, then a French possession, at a rate of around 30,000 a year. The Dutch shipped Africans to Surinam; the Portuguese transported them to Brazil.

Hotbeds of rebellion

Slave revolts broke out everywhere, and they were often bloodily suppressed, as in Surinam in 1728 and Jamaica in 1760. In 1791 an insurrection was declared in Haiti, where half a million Africans were working. The

Top left
Freed slave, 1794. Drawing by Desrais, print by Montaland

Above
The slave trade. Print by Rollet, after Morland, 1794.

island, which accounted for almost half of the world's coffee production, was set ablaze and France had to

Left
Jean-Baptiste
Debret, *Brazilian
overseers thrashing
their slaves*. All ill
treatment was
authorised in the
case of
disobedience.

Bottom left
*Slave burdened with
a weight attached*

*by a chain to her
ankle*. Print by
Tardieu.

Background
*16 September 1802:
Negroes' revolt in
Santo Domingo
(Antilles)*. Print
by Pourvoyeur,
after Martinet.

and in 1850 it became the world's leading coffee producer, with an output of 150,000 tons. It only abolished slavery in 1889, a few years before it confronted its first major crisis of over-production.

surrender its position as foremost coffee producer to Holland. Slavery in French colonies was abolished in 1794 following pressure from the revolutionaries, only to be reinstated by Napoleon, under the influence of the Empress Josephine, who came from an important colonial family in Martinique. Forced labour was not abolished in Java until 1860; in Brazil, which gained independence in 1822, slaves continued to work in intolerable conditions,

Left
François Biard,
*The Abolition of
slavery in the
French colonies
in 1848*.
1849, châteaux of
Versailles and
Trianon.
Abolished during
the Revolution,
slavery was
reintroduced
under the
Empire.

The lands of green gold

Every coffee has its particular origins, and every coffee land its own working methods, standards of quality, yields and prices. Before it is roasted at its final destination, green coffee ripens in tropical countries, often ensuring a significant proportion of their revenue and playing an essential role in their balance of trade.

The coffee belt

Cultivated in over sixty-five countries spread over five continents, coffee is today produced in the entire inter-tropical zone to the north and south of the equator, up to 30° of latitude. Coffee growing accounts for a total of around eleven million hectares of the planet's surface area.

THE KING OF COFFEE

As leader in the output of Arabicas and runner-up in that of Robustas, Brazil has been the undisputed front-runner for over a century, with two million hectares planted with coffee, mainly in the state of Minas Gerais and the São Paulo region. Ever since 1900 periodic crises of over-production have sometimes led to massive destruction of excess stock. Even today, Brazil remains the foremost indicator of trends in prices: a climatic catastrophe like frost – which occurs every fifteen or twenty years – is enough to make the worldwide prices of coffee plummet drastically. These days 85% of Brazil's plantations grow Arabicas – representing almost a third of the global Arabica production scale. Two-thirds of Brazilian coffees are reserved for export, and most of the remainder is converted into soluble products in situ.

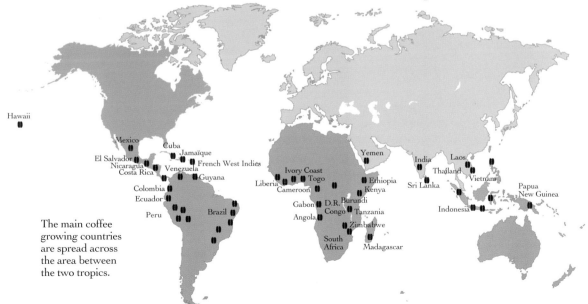

The main coffee growing countries are spread across the area between the two tropics.

FROM THE AMERICAS TO THE SHORES OF ASIA

The other Arabica producers of South and Central America are Colombia, Mexico, Guatemala, Costa Rica and Honduras, together responsible for some of the world's finest coffee. The coffee industry still thrives in Martinique and Guadeloupe, while the volcanic slopes of St. John's Peak in Jamaica are home to the most expensive coffee of all, the legendary Blue Mountain. In Africa, Ethiopia and Kenya are among the top Arabica producers. Asia

mainly concentrates on growing Robustas, with the exception of India, whose south-eastern Karnataka region cultivates both Arabicas and Robustas. Outstanding coffees can also be found on Pacific islands like Hawaii, as well as in Papua New Guinea. Indonesia is the main producer of Robustas, with about 20% of the total output, but in 1998 Vietnam, a latecomer to the coffee-growing club, turned out 300,000 tonnes of a very respectable coffee

that is more consistent than that of its neighbour. Sub-Saharan Africa, traditionally a supplier of full-bodied, medium-quality Robustas, has been making gradual progress: Ivory Coast, Uganda and Cameroon offer fairly cheap coffees, which often prove essential to their economic livelihood: Uganda, for example, obtains more than 90% of its foreign currency from coffee!

Green coffee production

(000 bags, 2003)

ARABICAS		ROBUSTAS	
Brazil	19,637	Vietnam	11,250
Colombia	11,750	Brazil	8,823
Mexico	4,550	Indonesia	5,384
Ethiopia	4,333	India	3,046
Guatemala	3,465	Uganda	2,697

Arabicas account for 70% of the total production of green coffee. In 1825 the entire world output of coffee came to around 2 million bags; in 2003, enough was collected to fill 102 million bags!

Work all the year round

"Coffee growing is a type of farming where you can never rest on your laurels, it constantly keeps you on tenterhooks. There is always something to do in a coffee field."

(*Karen Blixen,* Out of Africa)

THE DIVERSITY OF PLANTATIONS

It is very difficult to describe a coffee plantation: indeed, what is there in common between a large hacienda run like an industrial empire and a small family farm? Generally speaking, the biggest plantations are found in Brazil, which has vast areas at its disposal and cultivates coffee on flat plateaus. In hilly regions, however, the reduced surface area of the land sometimes makes it necessary to create terraces, and the poor yields mean that coffee growing remains confined to traditional communities.

THE ORGANISATION OF A COFFEE PLANTATION

Every plantation is endowed with a greenhouse to ensure that plants reproduce. On a traditional farm, cuttings are then taken. In a more industrialised setting, laboratories supply plantules obtained by *in vitro* fertilisation or cloning. When the terrain permits, the young trees are planted in rows, with spaces of one to three metres between them, depending on the variety. (This

Above and right The young coffee plant is first allowed to grow in shade, on very rich compost inside a greenhouse. The shoots are then transplanted into plastic bags, one by one, before being placed in the plantation when they are of sufficient size.

Top right This Guatemalan stamp illustrates the different stages of growth of a coffee tree, from propagation to the production of cherries.

amounts to between 1,200 and 10,000 trees per hectare.) Hedges of higher trees are used to shelter them from sunlight, as well as serving as a windbreak. Yields can vary enormously: 125 kg/hectare from the poor soils of Africa; 250 kg/hectare from the leached earth of Cuba – but four tons/hectare on the lateritic slopes of Costa Rica! Work on a plantation is

spread out over the entire year to obtain a decent crop, but it is still a very labour-intensive process: the soil must be hoed and sometimes irrigated; the trees must be pruned, given fertilisers and treated against insects and diseases, etc. Ideally, the ultimate aim is to combine maximum yields with optimum quality, but it is sometimes difficult for planters to be really motivated by the latter, as they do not know the eventual fate of their product, whose flaws and virtues will only become clear at the roasting stage.

Left
Harvesting by hand in Zimbabwe.

Bottom left
A one-year-old coffee plant protected by a wooden frame.

The future of organic coffee

Even in regions traditionally devoted to large plantations, the organic cultivation of coffee has begun to strike a chord in growers with environmental concerns and enthusiasms. Guatemala, Mexico, Costa Rica, Peru, El Salvador and even Ethiopia have in some places turned back to natural manure and abandoned pesticides. In contrast, a lack of control is evident in some plantations, and a coffee can bear traces of a product prohibited ten years earlier, where stocks have yet to be exhausted...

Although the coffees of black Africa cannot aspire to an organic classification, they can generally be considered fairly pure, simply because their producers do not have the means for expensive treatments.

Harvest time

After being harvested, ripe coffee cherries are subjected to treatments of varying complexity or cost, depending on the initial quality of the variety produced – and the results desired.

BY HAND OR BY MACHINE

There are several ways of gathering coffee cherries. The first is totally manual and involves, at a given moment, collecting only the cherries that are fully ripe. As coffee fruits have the peculiarity of not all ripening at the same time, this makes it necessary to pass along the rows of tree several times during the ripening process.

COSTA RICA 45 cts.

This method, called selective picking, is obviously reserved for the best coffees – the ones intended to supply washed Arabicas. To simplify this task, in the case of less pampered coffees, a kind of large comb is run through the branches, taking with it all the fruit on the branch, both red and green, and often a good few leaves as well. This much less costly technique, known as stripping, is suited to Robustas or Arabicas that are going to remain natural. On very large plantations, especially in Brazil, a machine can be used: this moves along the lines of trees and shakes them so that the ripest fruits fall off.

Coffee harvesting is a long process that requires great attention to detail and day-by-day control of the cherries: an excess of green cherries, or of fruit left too long on the branch, will spoil

The picking method: only the very ripe cherries are gathered. This first selection will be followed by harvesting staggered over several days.

the taste of the coffee as they will pass their unpleasant taste on to the rest of the beans in the drying process. On coffee plantations, the cherries are gathered in large bags that are immediately taken to special treatment facilities on the back of a mule or by lorry. Some small-scale producers hand over their entire crop to a co-operative.

Below
The uniform red colour of these cherries indicates a crop picked by hand.

WASHED COFFEES

All the prestigious coffees are then treated by means of a so-called "wet" method that requires copious amounts of water. The harvested cherries are first soaked overnight in a tank of water, in order to swell and soften them. They then pass through a machine called a pulpier, which mechanically removes a large part of the skin and viscous pulp surrounding the beans. The waste from this operation is eliminated by means of powerful jets of water. The beans, still partly covered by pulp, are put into tanks to ferment, thereby speeding up the disintegration of the pulp. They are then dried

in order to remove their thin silver skin; this takes about ten days, if they are left out in the sun, although drying machines can complete the process in a mere three days. Once they are dry, the beans are passed through a husking machine. Colombia is the world's leading producer of washed coffees. These are almost always Arabicas, and they have a distinctive, easily recognisable sweetness.

Left
Just after the harvest (here in Burundi), the coffee cherries are rinsed with plenty of water and cleaned of soil and leaves.

NATURAL DRYING

The "dry" method is less

Above
Drying coffee in Zanzibar.

complicated and, above all, considerably less expensive. It is applied to almost all Robustas and some Arabicas, which are classified as natural – Brazil specialises in these. Naturally dried Arabicas have a more full-bodied taste than their washed counterparts. As soon as the cherries are harvested they are spread in a thin layer in the sun; they are turned over regularly so that the entire surface can benefit from the heat. After a month, the sun will have completely dried the pulp of the cherry, so all that is required is to pass them through a husking machine to obtain the beans.

Whatever drying method is used, once the green coffee beans have been removed from their silver skin they are then sieved and sorted – to rid them of dust and pebbles – before being calibrated

The search for perfection

For many years, researchers have been attempting to create the ideal coffee tree, as sturdy as a Robusta but with beans as tasty as those of the Arabica. At one point the solution seemed to be at hand: the Arbusta, a new hybrid obtained by crossing the two types. This new plant, suited to cultivation on plains, was mainly tried out in Ivory Coast but had to be discarded after a few years; it grew well but on reaching maturity its branches dropped so much that they needed supports.

Whatever method is used, the beans are always left to dry in the sun and then inspected.

and graded according to their size. It
must be verified that none of the beans
are rotten – just one bad bean can
contaminate an entire bag! Several of
these operations can now be performed
electronically but the final inspection,
just before the coffee is put in its bag, is
always left to specialists.

HARVESTING SEASONS

Coffee trees often flower several times
a year, so it is not unusual to harvest
the fruit twice a year. The harvesting season obviously varies
according to the country: buyers of green coffee schedule their
purchases in accordance with the different harvesting periods.

COUNTRY	HARVESTING SEASON
Brazil	June to September
Colombia	Almost all the year
Central America	October to March
Ivory Coast	November to April
Kenya	April to June; December and January
Vietnam	October to December
Indonesia	March to April October to January

	WASHED ARABICAS	NATURAL ARABICAS	WASHED ROBUSTAS	NATURAL ROBUSTAS
Percentage	44%	32%	1%	22%
Producing countries	Colombia, Central America, Caribbean	Mainly Brazil (99%)	Indonesia (Java), India	Africa (50%), South-East Asia (50%)

It is worth knowing whether
a coffee comes from the
beginning or end of a
harvesting season, as this
affects the taste (more acid at
first, more bitter later on).

On the trail of the great vintages

J̶ust as the soil of a vineyard influences the personality of a wine, every coffee with a label guaranteeing its origin reflects the soil on which it was grown. Although most of the Arabicas on the market are more or less standardised mixtures, connoisseurs can still enjoy the authentic taste of some regional coffees.

Coffee terminology

As in oenology, coffeeology – this neologism does exist – has its own vocabulary, albeit very similar to that of wine. The "body" can be light, medium or full. The aromas of coffee – and there are hundreds of them! – can be musty, floral, wild.... A further host of adjectives describe the taste: nutty, smoky, earthy, zesty, winy, buttery, spicy, tangy. The acidity, the signature of a truly great coffee, is often only moderately appreciated by non-experts: it ranges from low to high. The smoothness and aftertaste of a brew are also taken into account. As with wines, a good vintage can be clean, rich, fine, smooth or lively, while a poor coffee can be astringent, flat, sour or scorched. Finally, and very importantly, a gourmet coffee must be a combination of several virtues: it can then be considered complete and balanced.

Outstanding vintages

Sidamo. As the ancestor of all the Arabicas on earth, Ethiopian Moka deserves to be mentioned first. It comes in a variety of forms, and it is best to be wary of the Moka classification, which is applied to both washed and natural coffees. The best Moka vintage is undoubtedly the Sidamo, which is grown on small terraced plantations in southern Ethiopia. When fresh this fine, washed coffee gives off a delicious fragrance of hot apricots. Ethiopia also produces another washed Moka, the Limu, and a natural Arabica, the Harrar.

Blue Mountain from Jamaica. Extolled as much as it is denigrated, Blue Mountain is a somewhat light, sweet, aromatic coffee that is considered flat by its detractors. It is very delicate and cannot endure being prepared in Espresso. Its extremely high price obviously reflects its quality, but also its scarcity – very little is produced – and its appeal to connoisseurs, particularly in Japan.

Supremo from Colombia. This washed Arabica, derived from the plants grown in the French West Indies in the 18th century, provides a balanced brew with a very smooth taste and low acidity.

Maragogypes from Mexico. These giant beans give the best results when they are grown on the mountain slopes overlooking the Pacific. Their quality is irregular, but at best they result in a balanced, fragrant coffee.

Tournon from Costa Rica, from large,

Opposite, top left
Advertisement for Indian coffee, 19th century, Library of Decorative Arts. South-East India has extensive coffee plantations in the Mysore region and along the Malabar Coast.

Opposite, bottom
An assortment of coffees with different colours, in their jute bags.

Above
Ethiopian Moka is the ancestor of all the Arabicas that are grown today.

The exception to the rule: Blue Mountain from Jamaica, the world's most expensive coffee, is stored in barrels rather than bags.

New coffees, new dangers

The last few years have witnessed the emergence of "sun-grown" coffees that do not require shade. This development has its advantages: trees can be planted closer together, making work easier and increasing productivity. The results are difficult to evaluate, and vary according to the species, but increased output can be matched with a noticeable reduction in the calibre of the beans. Evaporation must also be taken into account, as this increases when coffee trees cease to enjoy the benefit of shade. In the long term, the greatest risk in some areas involves the leaching of the soil: although there is little to fear on deep, fertile ground, there is a danger from the exhausting monoculture of high-yield coffee trees on poor land. Sun-grown coffee should therefore be reserved for plantations at high altitudes with slopes shrouded in cloud cover.

bluish-green beans, comes from extraordinarily fertile, volcanic soils. It is full-bodied, aromatic and balanced.
Antigua from Guatemala is another great vintage from Central America. It is grown at altitude and is fairly full-bodied, with a high acidity and often a chocolaty taste. à la saveur souvent chocolatée.
Kenya AA, rivals Sidamo as the best African Arabica, and is certainly one of the best in the world, with a fairly high acidity and a highly distinctive, fine, fruity taste.
Hawaii Kona. Little known, and unfortunately suffering from declining production, Kona is twice as cheap as Blue Mountains and, according to some experts, superior in

quality: fine and aromatic, it is more full-bodied than its Jamaican rival.
Sigri from New Guinea. Its full body and highly acid taste make it a coffee highly prized by connoisseurs.

Malabar from India is exposed to monsoon rains for several weeks, enhancing its peppery aromas and giving it a beautiful yellow tone.

And the rest…

Brazil, El Salvador, Java and Yemen all grow coffees that may be less prestigious but are nonetheless worthy of mention. Just a brief visit to a coffee wholesaler gives some idea of the mind-boggling diversity of coffee beans. They can be small or giant, yellow or silvery, with a blue or green glimmer; there are hundreds of grades, depending on their origin and their quality.

Opposite
Every producing country has its own, easily distinguishable bags.

Right
Every coffee has its own particular beans. They are all different, both in size and colour.

Have bag, will travel

Once green coffee has been sorted, calibrated and made ready for its long journey to the cup, it packed into jute bags at a standardised rate of 60 kilos. Before finding a buyer, it must be graded once more according to scrupulous criteria, before being tasted by an expert jury.

THE SCENT OF COFFEE
Right from the plantation, coffees are meticulously graded on the basis of any possible defects: are there any imperfect, dry or damaged beans? Black or fermented ones? Are there any still with husks? These qualitative criteria are further complicated by consideration of the size of the bean. Every country has its own grading system that precisely defines the quality of the beans that are put on sale.

And then, how to go about choosing a coffee? Plunging one's nose into a bag of beans is pointless: green coffee has no smell! Aromas only emerge with roasting. Coffee can, however, pick up various smells en route: for example, coffee that is delayed in the port of Rio de Janeiro and exposed to the spray off the Atlantic is said to be *rioy*, while Indian beans that absorb the violent rains of the monsoon through the jute are *monsooned*. The famous Blue Mountain from Jamaica is not transported in

Above and top
Once it has been treated, green coffee is put into jute bags and then loaded on to the ships that take it to the consuming countries.

Right, below
Sampling coffees in a major trading company.

bags: uniquely, it is sent on its way in oak barrels. In the past, however, casks that had previously been used to mature rum were used; the smell persisted in the wood and impregnated the coffee with a mellow aroma.

It is precisely this receptivity of the green bean to outside smells that makes vigilance necessary in both storage and transportation. Many a good coffee has been polluted by a slight musty taste acquired during an overlong stopover on a dock.

Above
Stack of coffee bags. The storage area must be ventilated and kept at a constant temperature, to avoid any risk of disease or mildew.

CUPPING

In coffee jargon, a professional taster is known as a "cupper". Before the newly harvested beans can be sold and dispatched, they must be cupped. This operation is repeated several times by different cuppers, both in the country of origin – before sale – and on arrival at the coffee's final destination, to monitor the quality of the disembarked batch and check that it matches the sample that has been supplied beforehand. Coffee cupping is governed by immutable and internationally recognised rules. Each member of the jury is presented with cups filled with ground coffee steeped in water; by each cup, there is a handful of green coffee and another of roasted coffee. The tasting takes place "blind", without any indication of the coffee's origins, leaving the cupper to make an assessment of the qualities and defects of each specimen.

The price of coffee

Coffee is a strategic product, second only to oil in trading levels. Since 1882, the date of the first transaction on the New York Coffee Exchange, coffee has been listed on the spot market, with its prices being subject to the general regulations for forward markets.

Below
A pyramid of coffee bags in

São Paulo, Brazil.

COFFEE DEALING

By the 19th century, dealers had acquired their own fleets of clippers that loaded up with coffee in tropical ports. Substantial profits were made, but a paucity of information often made it difficult for coffee growers to negotiate the purchase price of their produce. Moreover, the coffee trade involved real risks.

Above
Speculation with coffee preceded the creation of a specific Exchange, as this print from 1866 demonstrates.

In order to regulate the market and protect its participants, the Coffee Exchange was created in the 1880s, and the figure of the coffee dealer gradually became associated with great technical expertise. Since then, dealers who have remained aloof from conglomerations of coffee merchants and the mass production of the multinationals have come to play an essential role as they can offer their customers – often small- or medium-scale coffee roasters -– all types of coffee, all the year round, in whatever quantities are desired. Such dealers never buy less than one container of coffee, but they have to sell it bag by bag.

FLUCTUATIONS IN PRICES

Although coffee has been perfectly stable in terms of production and consumption for a decade or so, its stock market has experienced significant fluctuations. The price is obviously affected by the state of world stocks and harvesting conditions: prices soared when frost hit Brazil (1994); they also went up in panic when Cyclone Mitch tore through the plantations of Central America (1998) and when an earthquake shook Colombia (1999). Nevertheless, fluctuations in price are more often caused by natural disasters than by speculation. The presence of common investment funds in forward markets, particularly in the United States, has the advantage of providing liquid assets, but it also tends to exaggerate the number of movements. The "paper market" therefore greatly exceeds the real market, so that in New York it represents every year the equivalent of twenty or thirty times the world harvest. There have even been cases of 25,000 bags of coffee being bought and resold in a single day.

Below
In the early 1930s, Brazil had to confront an overproduction of over 6 million bags of coffee per year. Some of it was dumped in the sea, the rest mixed with tar to serve as fuel for steam trains.

Right
The international Arabica Coffee Exchange was located in the World Trade Center, New York.

The Coffee Exchanges

Robustas are listed in London, in dollars per tonne. The minimum batch bought is five tonnes, or around eighty-five bags, but most transactions involve a minimum of fifteen tonnes – the contents of a container.

Arabicas are traded on the Coffee Exchange in New York, which was formerly situated on the seventh floor of the World Trade Center. The listings are fixed in cents (of American dollars) per pound in weight. A batch of Arabicas comprises two hundred and fifty bags, or just under 15 tons.

The secrets
of black gold

Roasting coffee is apparently nothing more than a simple matter of grilling the beans. And yet... there is as much difference between green beans and a roasted coffee as there is between flour and freshly baked bread: if the roasting is insufficient or excessive, or clumsily performed, even the best beans can be spoiled beyond repair.

Changes in state

When coffee is roasted its chemical composition is modified. These changes determine what it will look like and, once aromas develop, how it will taste.

Below
The burning coffee comes out of the roaster in one go and must then be cooled in the air.

Top right
Advertisement for a coffee merchant in Paris, 1867. Carnavalet Museum.

AT THE HEART OF THE BEAN
First of all, every coffee bean contains... water! More than 12% of its weight is comprised of humidity, which disappears almost completely during the roasting process. Plenty of other elements also play a role in its composition, but these partly depend on the variety, the growing method – some chemical treatments can leave traces – and the ripeness of the berry when it is picked. The elements hidden in the hollows of beans may prove surprising: sugars and acids, proteins, fats, alkaloids – including the famous caffeine – and even mineral salts (particularly potassium, but also magnesium and calcium). Some elements disappear under the effect of heat, while others combine to form complex fusions. Those elements that are not soluble in water obviously do not reach the cup.

Below
Coffee beans: natural; roasted

a "capuche" colour; grilled Italian style.

CHAIN REACTIONS

The most visible change in coffee through roasting involves the pigmentation: the bean gradually turns an ochre colour, then brown or almost black. The loss of water causes a drop in weight of around 20%, while volume increases through the heat. Sucrose levels go down, along with the general acidity, but the caffeine level rises slightly. The water and sugars combine to form a caramel. When the temperature is about 200° C the acids in the coffee, known as the "precursors" of aromas", react together and various aromas emerge, only to be destroyed by the carbonisation.

A coffee roaster must take all these factors into account to calculate the precise endpoint of the process: the sooner the roasting is completed, the higher the acidity of the coffee; the more it is prolonged, the greater the bitterness. These calculations largely depend on the green coffee used and the eventual consumer.

Opposite
The coffee roaster carries out several controls during the roasting process by removing a few beans from the drum.

Profession: coffee roaster

The Arabs were the first to roast coffee, in the 14th century. For centuries, coffee was mainly roasted in the home or within the context of a local community, but now this delicate operation – essential to the preparation of high-quality coffees – is entrusted to professionals.

TIME-HONOURED CUSTOMS

The caravans that once crisscrossed Arabia used to carry in their luggage a simple utensil for roasting their coffee: a metal grill that stood on the ground over a log fire. Elsewhere, coffee was for years roasted in the kitchen: in *The Correct Use of Tea, Coffee and Chocolate*, published in 1687, Nicolas de Blégny recommends putting the beans "in a tinned copper basin over a blazing fire", without forgetting to "stir continuously with an iron instrument". Right up to the early 20th century, many European families still roasted their own coffee: in *Claudine's House* Colette described how the air in her mother's kitchen was fragrant with coffee whenever she roasted some beans. The preference for caracolis in the north of France can be traced back to home roasting: the roundness of the bean made it easier to cook evenly in a simple frying pan.

Right
Title page of the book written by the King's doctor, Nicolas de Blégny, on *The Correct Use of Tea, Coffee and Chocolate for their preservation and for curing illnesses*, 1687.

LE BON USAGE
DU THE'
DU CAFFE'
ET
DU CHOCOLAT
POUR LA PRESERVATION
& pour la guerison des
Maladies.

Par Mr DE BLEGNY, Conseiller, Medecin Artiste ordinaire du Roy & de Monfieur, & prépofé par ordre de fa Majefté, à la Recherche & Vérification des nouvelles découvertes de Medecine.

A PARIS,
Chez ESTIENNE MICHALLET, ruë
S. Jacques, à l'Image S. Paul.

M. DC. LXXXVII.
Avec Approbation & Privilege du Roy.

Au PLANTEUR DU PIRANGA A. PICARD Cafés brûlés 4, Rue Pajol, PARIS.

Above
An advertisement for a Parisian coffee-roasting shop.

Right
A traditional method for roasting coffee, in a Moroccan street in 1945.

The coffee-roasting market

In countries like France or Italy, where coffee forms part of a long-standing tradition, the more humble roasters are fighting to survive against extremely strong international competition. In France, for example, 85% of today's market is effectively in the hands of multinationals with a wide range of interests. Family businesses are still irreplaceable, however, because they offer a choice of original high-quality coffees at varying prices, as opposed to the standardised products of big distributors.

THE FIRST COFFEE-ROASTING SHOPS

In the 18th century, when coffee drinking had become widespread in Europe, the first shops with colonial products began to appear. They sold tea, spices and, naturally, coffee. The shopkeepers bought their green beans from dealers and roasted them as required. The coffees they offered were often "house blends" made from available stocks, and each country developed tastes influenced by the deliveries received from their particular colonies: France, having first enjoyed coffee from the Caribbean, then became accustomed to Robustas of dubious quality from her African possessions.

Coffee-roasting shops were often passed on from father to son, acquiring over the years a family know-how that is still evident today. In France some seven hundred "small" coffee roasters are still in operation, the vast majority also owning a retail outlet. Some have diversified their activity and sell their products to cafés or restaurants, or have their own coffee rooms, in which customers can sample a cup before buying a packet.

Left, top
A coffee-roasting shop in Paris, in the early twentieth century.

Left, bottom
Advertising for "Moka à la française", sold by Paul Mairesse in Cambrai.

Right
Once coffee is taken out of a roaster, it must be stirred in the air to stop it cooking any longer.

Whether packed in an airtight bag or an hermetic can, coffee must preserve its freshness impeccably.

The rules of packaging

The preservation of coffee is a constant battle for a coffee-roaster. Whereas green coffee, with its high water content, tends to absorb all the smells around it through the bag, roasted coffee quickly loses its aromatic qualities if it is not protected from humidity, light and air.

Leaving beans to rest

Freshly roasted coffee must not be drunk straight away – it needs to rest for a day or two after this traumatic process. Newly roasted beans in effect continue to "work" for at least twenty-four hours, and they cannot be put on sale until the gases trapped in the beans are spontaneously released. The coffee industry has perfected a device specifically for this purpose, in the form of a bag fitted with a valve; this one-way opening is vital, as it allows the gases to leave but blocks the entrance of air.

Ground coffees

These days, buying coffee in the form of beans is almost exclusively confined to restaurants. Few domestic buyers continue this practice, and 80% of retail sales involve ground coffee. The choice of appropriate packaging is therefore crucial as, once a coffee has been ground, it must be kept under suitable conditions; if not, even the best vintage can turn into an insipid or rancid powder in a few days. In most cases ground coffees are sold in blends. On being taken from the mill, various beans are mixed together and then put into airtight packaging. This is usually the classic packet, sealed under vacuum. Once the packet has been opened, the coffee must be used quickly, in less than a week, and preferably kept in the refrigerator. Some coffee suppliers prefer other types of packaging, such as an hermetically closed metal can, which is certainly more appropriate but also more expensive.

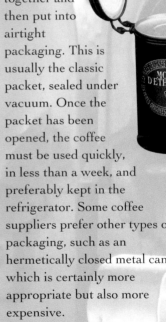

Packets of many colours

In order to make it easier for the consumer to choose, a coffee user's code has developed over time, based on different colours. Red, therefore, traditionally designates the full-bodied coffees that are most suited to morning time: the bright colour suggests awakening – and the presence of Robusta in the blend. The colour black signals a high-quality Arabica coffee; it also frequently

denotes a vintage without any blending.

Gold generally marks the highpoint of a brand, while soothing blue indicates decaffeinated coffee intended for night-time consumption. Some coffee suppliers have opted for a touch of fantasy, by offering highly original packaging tinged with exoticism for their more unusual products.

In principle, a coffee supplier has total freedom as regards packaging, but in practice the market has strict rules aimed at helping the consumer make a choice.

The real price of coffee

A coffee grower sets a price that takes into account the production costs; this serves as a bottom line that is indexed on the market price. The dealer collects the green coffee on the agreed date and stores it in warehouses, in the hope of selling it to his clientele of coffee suppliers at a price that covers costs and also leaves a profit.

The coffee supplier goes on to resell it, bearing in mind the factory expenses, the loss of merchandise during the roasting, the packaging costs and the advertising budget. In all this time the coffee has become about seven times more expensive, meaning that a vintage coffee sold at a retail outlet can cost £60 per kilo or more. This price primarily depends on the scarcity of the vintage in question, however, and a Blue Mountain can easily be put on sale at £300 per kilo…

From the corner shop to the factory

The difference between a coffee roaster who grills beans in a backroom behind his shop and a large factory processing hundreds of tonnes of beans every day is not merely one of scale. They use different methods, and this is reflected in the results.

THE TRADITIONAL METHOD

Coffee retailers who roast their own products generally work with batches of around twenty-five kilos. The green beans are put into a roasting machine comprising a drum fitted with an axis and heated by gas. When the beans are tossed about inside the drum, they are licked by the gas flames and roasted slowly, for twenty minutes, at a temperature of almost 200° C. An air current sucks up the thin film that is now coming away from the beans. As the operation advances, the brazing of the beans produces a distinctive crackling sound; at this point, master roasters draw on their experience to assess the progress of the roasting by ear. A small probe can be introduced into the drum to confirm the diagnosis. When the roasting is considered optimal, the darkened beans are taken out and left to cool in the air. The slowness of the process is essential to preserving the delicacy of Arabicas, whilst also ensuring that the beans are cooked right through. Some medium-size roasting companies still use this traditional method for their gourmet coffees, which come in smaller batches.

THE FAST METHOD

More powerful machines are used when large quantities are being handled. These are capable of roasting four hundred kilograms of beans in about ten minutes. The coffee is kept in suspension in extremely hot air (800° C) inside

Right
A small-scale roaster used in the traditional treatment of beans.

an enormous conical receptacle. A minimum of eight minutes is enough to ensure the completion of the chemical reactions required to produce the aromas. The beans are then exposed to the air and stirred to cool. This method, which was developed for coffees destined for large-scale distribution, provides consistent and acceptable results, but is not applicable to sophisticated vintages.

Instant coffees

Instant coffee is obtained by total dehydrating the roasted bean, which is transformed into a highly concentrated solid. When the coffee comes out of the roasting machine, it is ground and then prepared in a percolator. The resulting liquid is dehydrated in heat, or lyophilised in cold under a vacuum. Fairly full-bodied coffees are used for these techniques. Many Brazilian and African Robustas are treated in this way in situ, in specially built instant-coffee factories.

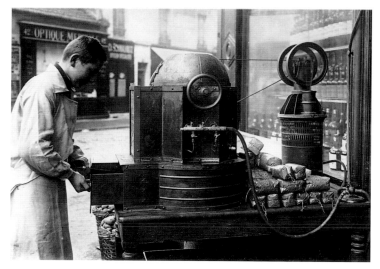

THE HOT-AIR METHOD

Only unexceptional Robustas can survive this extra-fast method, capable of roasting many tons of coffee in an hour. The beans are subjected to an intensely hot blast of air for one and a half minutes. This technique is far too aggressive to bring out any complexity of aroma, but it does serve to churn out the beans that are used for the ground blends found in instant and lyophilised coffees.

Left
A coffee roaster in 1919: the machine is run by a hot-air engine.

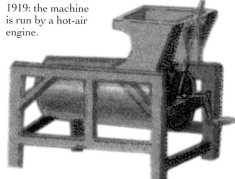

The art of blending

Just as champagne winegrowers take a selection of their wines to make a specific vintage, in the same way coffee roasters choose, taste and assemble their own delicious and well-balanced blends.

Below
Smaller machines are used for reduced quantities.

Above right
Interior of Verlet Coffees, Paris.

TASTE AND AROMAS

Both coffee shops and roasting factories are immediately distinguished by the same omnipresent – and mouth-watering – smell of freshly roasted coffee. A coffee does have to live up to this promise in the cup, however. This is perhaps the most difficult task of all, as our taste buds are not accustomed to detecting more than a few flavours: acidity, bitterness and sometimes a touch of saltiness. There is a risk of disappointment, as a well-trained nose is capable of isolating almost one thousand aromas!

READING THE LABELS

A coffee label reading "100% Arabica" unfortunately leaves many questions unanswered. Are they washed or natural Arabicas? What procedures were used to grow and select the cherries, and how ripe were they at harvest time? What roasting method was used? How was the coffee ground? Is the packaging airtight? Labels do not provide enlightenment on such matters – and if they did, they might produce some surprises. A good coffee merchant normally has a stock of around twenty pure vintages, and three or

four blends from recipes that are kept secret. It is customary to call a mixture that contains some Robustas a "full-bodied blend", while "Pure Arabica" is applied to other cases. Companies that prepare coffees for large-scale distribution operate in the same way: they have their own special blend. Pricing policies and competition lead them to select the most affordable beans, which often include mass-produced, natural Brazilian Arabicas. It is vital that they can offer their customers the same taste under the same label, regardless of the vicissitudes of a particular year's output, which cannot be allowed to prevent a company from continuing to put the same packet of coffee on the market. It therefore has to find a new recipe every year to adapt to any changes in the raw material and ensure that the taste does not change.

The perfect coffee...

...is obviously a matter of taste! Although plenty of suppliers entice their customers with such an offer, this reiteration must be interpreted as a tribute to diversity: what would be sadder than a standard flavour common to all coffees? There are, however, a few basic tips that will allow anybody – even a domestic buyer keen to create a personal blend – to obtain what connoisseurs describe as a "complete" coffee: a touch of Brazil for sweetness, of Colombia for delicacy, of Costa Rica for body, of Mexico for acidity, etc. No exceptional vintage will be found in these mixtures, as they would be drowned in a blend and deserve to be drunk on their own.

Black or
white?

Taking care when buying coffee does not guarantee the quality of the beverage made with it. The next step is to prepare it with equal care. The water, the grinding and the coffee-maker all play their part, along with individual tastes and the time of day.

From beans into powder

Coffee beans were once ground by hand in a wooden mortar or reduced to powder in a spice mill, but nowadays they are more uniformly processed with electric grinders.

FOR COLLECTORS ONLY

The emergence of the custom of coffee drinking brought with it objects designed for its preparation. Jean de La Roque, the first man to bring coffee to Marseilles in the 17th century, took the precaution of also taking onboard a mill and coffee pot he had bought in Turkey. The Ottomans originally used the Arab pestle and mortar, and the coffee grinders in Istanbul even formed their own trade guild. These first mortars, made of turned wood and sometimes decorated with geometrical carvings, were later replaced by cylindrical, copper mills – and these were what the French used when they first started to drink coffee. A little later, mills with two sections began to appear: the top was fitted with a handle and a "nut" for grinding, the bottom was a receptacle with a drawer. The main materials used were wood (for the bottom) and metal (for the pieces on top), although the big mills set on restaurant counters were made of cast iron. Plenty of these old coffee mills have survived to this day: they are on display in museums of popular art or are snapped up by collectors.

Above
A double-wheel coffee mill for a counter. For many years this type of mill, widespread in the 19th century, was manufactured in France by Peugeot.

Left
Metal mill with a fluted bowl.

A CRUCIAL PROCESS

The importance of the method used to mill coffee has not always been fully appreciated, and in the 19th century it was not uncommon to find country folk drinking bad coffee that they had merely crushed and strained.

We are now fully aware that a bad mill can spoil the taste of a good coffee, by overheating the beans in an overlong operation or producing an irregular powder. The classic mills with blades present these problems. Domestic users who prefer to mill their own beans are best advised to use a grinder: this ensures a homogenous milling that takes nothing away from the aroma of the coffee. Another factor to take into account is the texture of the powder most appropriate for the coffee-maker being used: coarse, medium, fine or very fine.

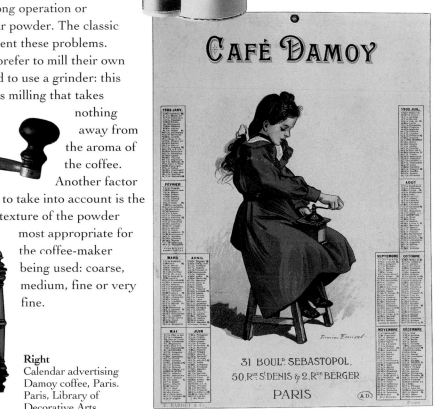

Opposite page, left
Travelling coffee mill, in copper covered with leather (late 18th century).

Opposite page, right
Turkish coffee mill, in copper decorated with crescent hallmarks.

Left
Modern coffee mill: Antigua model, Bodum brand.

Below
Flemish metal coffee mill with silver plate and gilt, early 19th century.

Right
Calendar advertising Damoy coffee, Paris. Paris, Library of Decorative Arts.

Making a good cup of coffee

A versatile object equally at home in a kitchen and on an elegant dining table, the coffee-maker obviously plays a key role in the preparation of a good brew. It can become so much an integral part of everyday life – whatever model is chosen – that it is one of the last things that many families would be willing to relinquish.

WATER FOR COFFEE

Generally served at breakfast or after a meal, coffee can be a gourmet's delight – provided, of course, that all the appropriate ingredients are in place. A disappointing brew cannot always be blamed on the coffee itself – the water must also be taken into account. If there is too much chlorine or lime, it is advisable to use slightly mineralised, bottled water. Another alternative, adopted by many restaurants, is to filter the water before it reaches the coffee-maker.

DECOCTION

The first coffee drinkers made an infusion with powder, as if they were making tea: the coffee was allowed to macerate for a few minutes in a receptacle filled with hot water. Many connoisseurs argue, however, that a boiled coffee is a spoiled coffee, although Oriental traditions have maintained the custom of boiling coffee at the same time as the water. With this method, cold water is poured into a small, copper coffee pot with two or three spoonfuls of very finely ground coffee, and often some sugar. It is brought slowly to the boil at least three times, stirring all the while to make the brew frothy. The coffee is served but is not drunk straight

Caffé Caffé

Below, left
Print from *New and curious treaty on coffee*, by P. S. Dufour, published in 1693.

Above
Illustration from *Studies of humble people or the cries of Paris*, Bouchardon, 1746.

away – the grounds must be
allowed to settle on the bottom of
the cup. According to the
geographical location, the
resulting beverage goes under
the name of Oriental, Turkish,
Arab, Greek or Moorish coffee.
Another technique developed by
the Mélior company just after
World War II was based on the
same principle, but the grounds
were removed before drinking:
the powdered coffee is infused
for a few minutes, then separated
from the liquid by means of a
plunger that pushes the grounds
to the bottom of the cylinder of
the coffee pot. The results are
quite acceptable if
very finely ground
coffee is used.

Right
Modern plunger
pot, Chambord
model, Bodum
brand.

Far right
Poster by René
Ravo to
advertise the
Mélior coffee
pot. Paris,
Forney Library.

CAFETIERE
Melior

Encore
meilleure

René
Ravo

Above
Series of classic china coffee pots. The filter is set on top of the pot.

Opposite
The two glass bowls of a press pot.

FILTRATION

The china coffee pot, the ancestor of all the objects used to prepare filtered coffee, is topped with a filter – also made of china – that is perforated with small holes. Fairly coarsely ground coffee is put in the filter, and barely simmering water is put on top. This type of coffee pot has two major disadvantages: firstly, the china retains the smell of previous coffees, which contaminates the taste of the brew; secondly, some of the grounds often pass through the filter – but this was solved by inserting a paper filter that collects the dregs. Modern electric coffee-makers are based on the same concept. The results are satisfactory as long as the coffee is stirred before it is served, to make the concentration more uniform.

Right
A state-of-the-art electric coffee-maker: the Crystal Aroma Plus by Moulinex.

Far right
Two in one: an electric coffee-maker and an Espresso machine, by Krups.

THE PRESS POT

Highly prized by connoisseurs, this coffee-maker combines stylishness with a respect for the aromas of coffee; it is often used to prepare delicate vintages that an Espresso machine would "burn". Made up of two transparent dark bowls linked by a tube and separated by a filter, it first appeared in England in the mid-19th century. Water is poured into the lower bowl and the coffee powder, which should be finely ground, is put in the "tulip" on top of it. The apparatus is then sealed with an airtight stopper. When the water is heated it goes up the tube into the coffee; when the heat is extinguished, the coffee comes slowly back down into the lower bowl, while the grounds are retained in the filter in the tulip.

THE ITALIAN COFFEE-MAKER

This type of coffee-maker, invented around fifty years ago (reputedly in Naples), can be found in most homes in Italy and many more in the rest of Europe. It is made up of two sections separated by a metal filter. Fairly finely ground coffee is put on top of the filter, and when the water below reaches a temperature of 100° C it percolates through the filter. A truly excellent cup of coffee can never be obtained this way: the steam that passes through the coffee burns the aromas, and the metal can be tasted in the final brew!

THE ESPRESSO MACHINE

This machine – designed, as its name suggests, to prepare coffee quickly – dates from the 19th century but only really became popular after World War II, thanks to some improvements made by a Milanese café-owner called Achille Gaggia. It can now be seen in most coffee-drinking countries, and in recent years has even experienced a boom in the major American cities. A good Espresso requires finely ground coffee, accurately measured – most countries establish a legal dose per cup – and suitably packed into the metal filter. Inside the machine, a pressure of at least ten bars brings the water temperature to 85-90° C – but absolutely no more than that! This can be difficult to control, and an excessive temperature burns the coffee and takes away much of its subtlety. The coffee's extraction time also has a part to play; if the water goes through too slowly, the coffee will be over-extracted and will have a burnt taste; if it goes through too quickly, the coffee will be weak and the whitish foam on top will not be frothy. The ideal Espresso has a velvety texture and attractive, amber-coloured foam.

Melitta's invention

In the early 20th century, Dresden witnessed the appearance of the paper filter, the fruit of the ingenious imagination of one Melitta Bentz. It occurred to her that she could prevent the grounds passing through the holes in her china coffee pot by covering them with blotting paper. Delighted with the results, she shrewdly set about marketing her invention. A hundred years later, Melitta's grandchildren are still running what is now an internationally renowned company.

THE IMPORTANCE OF THE DOSAGE

How much coffee should be used? Electric coffee machines have instructions printed on the filter holder. For other forms of preparation, counting is the best solution: one teaspoon per cup for Turkish coffee; about ten grams for a press pot, slightly less for an Espresso machine; and for a cup of filtered coffee, that depends on individual tastes – a quarter of an ounce is sufficient for an American-style brew, but a stronger, Continental-style cup requires almost double that. Espresso coffee is often criticised for the variations in quality from one cup to another: it only needs a slight excess of temperature, or powder ground a little too finely or packed too tightly, for the coffee to be ruined. It is now possible to buy machines that make it easy to prepare Espresso coffee, similar to that served in cafés, in only a few seconds with "pre-dosed" coffees, sold in aluminium or paper sachets. Although such a machine involves a considerable outlay, its speed and the uniformity of its results offer great advantages for connoisseurs who refuse to shirk quality but have little time to spare.

Top left
Honoré Daumier, *The coffee lover*, lithograph from the *Monomanes* series.

Above
A good Espresso is instantly recognisable, with its thick, uniform foam, neither too dark nor too light.

Left
Professional Espresso machine.

Opposite, top A fresh interpetation of the Neopolitan coffee-maker, by Riccardo Dalisi for Alessi.

Opposite, below In 1979, Alessi commissioned Richard Sapper to design the first coffee pot in the range. The 9090 model went on to worldwide success and was even displayed in the Museum of Modern Art in New York!

Passion and excess

"I never drink coffee – it stops me sleeping!" Many people have been put off by coffee because of its fame as a stimulant. Its reputation for awakening the intellectual faculties has, however, made it popular with a great many artists who have not hesitated to use it – and abuse it.

A friend to writers
Originally considered a medicine capable of curing all types of ailments, from the common cold to poor digestion, coffee soon provoked hostility, and its possible ill effects have

Left
Jean Baptiste Greuze, *Le Bovier Fontenelle* (Versailles Historical Museum). He was a great coffee drinker and lived to the age of 99.

aroused debate ever since. In the 18th century, however, admirers of Diderot noted that, according to his Encyclopaedia, coffee aided digestion and enhanced the intellectual capacities. As a result, contemporary men of letters were quick to drink copious amounts, and were amazed to find that they could work until late at night without feeling tired. Voltaire was undoubtedly one of the most famous coffee drinkers of the time. When the writer Bernard Le Bovier Fontenelle was approaching the age of 100, he gave the following reply to a well-wisher who advised him to cut back on his coffee consumption:

"I've been drinking it for 80 years, so it must be a poison with very slow effects if I am not yet dead!"

A "modern stimulant"
A century later, Honoré de Balzac devoted some extraordinary pages to the beverage, which became an essential part of his existence. In his *Treatise on modern stimulants*, he made a proclamation that, no doubt unwittingly, reads uncannily like an epitaph:

"Coffee is a roaster of the insides"

Balzac knew what he was talking about: his passion for coffee had gone beyond all

> "Many people attribute to coffee the power to imbue wittiness; but it's plain to see that boring people are even more boring after they have drunk it!"

Redoutable caffeine

Caffeine may be odourless, colourless and tasteless, but it has nothing in common with water! This alkaloid from the purine family, found not only in coffee but also in tea, chocolate and the coca plant, is a strong stimulant that is totally absorbed by the body. Once coffee is ingested, the caffeine passes immediately into the blood stream, but its maximum effect comes one hour later and it remains active for about another five hours. This is why some coffee drinkers can indulge in a cup just before going to bed: they go to sleep so quickly that the caffeine does not have enough time to take effect!

reasonable limits. He never allowed anybody else to go and buy his coffee (from two different merchants!) or to put together his favourite blend. Above all, he drank without any sense of moderation: this indefatigable worker, creator of a vast body of work, drank no less than fifty cups a day! He did, however, die exhausted at the age of fifty-one. Despite his enthusiasm, he derided coffee's supposed ability to sharpen the wits.

Top left
Honoré de Balzac, here photographed by Nadar, owned a coffee pot engraved with his initials.

Decaffeinated coffee

Many people who are susceptible to the effects of caffeine prefer to drink "decaf". This type of coffee is rid of its caffeine before roasting by means of a number of treatments, including soaking in a chemical bath followed by rinsing (the cheapest method), subjection to propane under pressure or successive rinses with water (a long process that requires huge amounts of water).

The varieties of coffee selected to make decaffeinated blends are, however, often of poor quality. Except in cases of an explicit medical prohibition, it is preferable to opt for a good Arabica with a low level of caffeine and prepare it, tightly packed, in an Espresso machine; contrary to expectations, this guarantees minimal levels of caffeine. Another alternative is simply to dilute the coffee in the cup with a little mineral water...

Above
Jean Huber, *The rising of Voltaire*. Paris, Carnavalet Museum. Voltaire wrote several texts denouncing the slave trade, but this did not diminish his enjoyment of coffee.

Below, right
Johann Sebastian
Bach Print by F.W. Nettling, after a painting by Gottlieb-Hausmann, 1746. Bach was a regular at the Zimmermann café in Lepizig, and it was there that the first performance of his famous *Coffee Cantata* was given in 1734.1746.

Musicians were also quick to investigate coffee. Beethoven used to count meticulously the number of beans required for the preparation of a good cup: 60. Rossini had some fanciful ideas about coffee: he was convinced that a few cups of coffee were all he needed to feel on top form for a few days, and that after that the effects wore off.

Dispelling some mistaken ideas

The world of coffee is distinguished by its great diversity. In some varieties, caffeine levels can soar disproportionately from a single coffee to a double one. It is therefore vital for particularly sensitive consumers to be aware of what they are drinking. A Sidamo Moka or a Brazilian

Coffee is a matter of 15 or 20 days, the time for making an opera
Rossini

very soluble in water, so its presence in the cup largely depends on the extraction time: the shorter this is, the less caffeine there will be. An Espresso machine passes water over the coffee very quickly, and it therefore produces coffees that are a great deal less caffeinated than those prepared by systems based on filtration.

Sul de Minas has a caffeine level of about 1.1%, a Hawaiian Kona 1.3%, a Blue Mountain 1.25%. All the Robustas have at least twice these amounts, which is why "full-bodied" blends should be reserved for the mornings, when their "kick" is best appreciated.

What is less well known is the fact that the preparation method considerably affects the caffeine content. Italian Espresso is often accused of being too "strong"; it is indeed strong in taste, but not in caffeine. In fact, caffeine is not

Top left
Rossini. Print on wood by Henry Duff Linton, after a drawing by Bocourt. Rossini was convinced that a few cups of coffee kept him on form for several days.

Right
A café overlooking the Bosporus near Istanbul; Pierre Loti liked to write here.

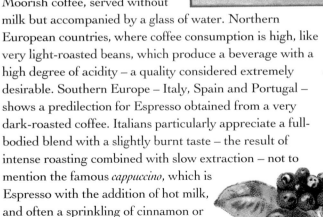

Different tastes and different colours

Full-bodied or smooth, strong or weak, black or white, with sugar or without: everybody has their own preference. And this diversity is just as it should be!

NATIONAL CUSTOMS…

Europe and the United States are great coffee consumers. The few drops of concentrated extract at the bottom of a tiny Italian cup are, however, a world away from the pints of coffee, reheated over the course of a day, drunk by many American families. The fact is that every country has its own habits, and these often form tastes that last a lifetime. North Africa and the Middle East are still attached to extremely sweet Moorish coffee, served without milk but accompanied by a glass of water. Northern European countries, where coffee consumption is high, like very light-roasted beans, which produce a beverage with a high degree of acidity – a quality considered extremely desirable. Southern Europe – Italy, Spain and Portugal – shows a predilection for Espresso obtained from a very dark-roasted coffee. Italians particularly appreciate a full-bodied blend with a slightly burnt taste – the result of intense roasting combined with slow extraction – not to mention the famous *cappuccino*, which is Espresso with the addition of hot milk, and often a sprinkling of cinnamon or nutmeg. Coffee does not enjoy a very good reputation in the United States: all too often Americans are content to drink

Above
An advertisement for Minot & Bastide biscuits sings the praises of *café au lait*.

Top left
Drinking Moorish coffee, chromatograph from the early 20th century.

sloppily prepared instant coffee. Meanwhile, England is tentatively rediscovering coffee after centuries of infatuation with tea. In Asia, Indonesians drink the Robusta that they themselves produce, while the Japanese, who came late to coffee, are prepared to pay out for the most expensive vintages.

...AND REGIONAL TASTES

Even within the same country, however, tastes in coffee vary from region to region, under the influence of the adjacent countries. For example, in France – where Espresso has generally long been reserved for bars and restaurants, while filtered coffee dominates in domestic settings – Northerners prefer a slightly acid coffee, to which they still sometimes add a little chicory. (It is often forgotten that Napoleon introduced chicory to replace the coffee that had become impossible to find during the Continental System.) They do not even mind rioy Brazilian coffee, which everybody else finds undrinkable. In Provence, the proximity of Italy has encouraged a taste for dark coffees. In the East, German customs have spread across the border, with a fondness for highly aromatic, acid Arabicas.

CHICORÉE EXTRA
MARQUE
A LA BELLE JARDINIÈRE

Names for coffees

What to order in a café? Coffee, obviously, such as an Espresso, which can be weak (with more water) or strong (more concentrated). This can be complemented by any number of additions: cold milk, hot milk, whipped cream (Viennese coffee), nutmeg or chocolate shavings, sugar, alcohol (a tot of brandy in Mediterranean countries, whisky in Irish coffee) or even vanilla syrup and ice cream (coffee frappé). Italian terms for coffee, such as cappuccino and Espresso, have entered into the pool of words that are instantly recognised all over the world.

Let's meet at the café

Oriental cafés where rendezvous are made more easily than at home, writers' cafés, artists' cafés, Viennese cafés with newspapers on the side, philosophers' cafés, revolutionary cafés, Bohemian cafés in Paris, quiet cafés ideal for a quick breather, subversive cafés where plots and coup d'états are hatched: the café is the perfect place to meet.

All the charm of the Orient

More than four centuries ago, a popular neighbour-hood in Istanbul witnessed the appearance of the first coffee houses. From the banks of the Bosporus it spread around the Mediter-ranean basin: this vital meeting place has sparked off a tradition that remains alive and well.

Below
The Oriental café is a place to meet and smoke a hookah. Café in Turkey, 1913.

IMANS AND CAFÉS

It was in the middle of the 16th century, around 1555, that the first café appeared, on the initiative of two Syrians who had settled in Istanbul. It quickly became popular as a meeting place for making business deals or relaxing with friends, and soon coffee houses were springing up all around the Golden Horn. In a country characterised by a reluctance to invite a stranger home, the ideal solution was to go out and have a drink together. Inevitably, the cafés soon aroused the suspicions of religious leaders: who knows what was being said at the back of these dimly-lit rooms? The imams, worried at the evidence of the abandonment of mosques in favour of these centres of pleasure and subversion, sought to ban the drink – to little avail: after only a few years, Istanbul boasted a total of over five hundred cafés!

THE WAVE OF ORIENTALISM

From the 17th century, coffee houses began to open in all the Mediterranean countries, and before long they could be

found all over Europe. Nothing, however, can rival the charm of the Oriental cafés. From Persia to Egypt to Algeria, there are countless humble taverns on the edge of the desert or on the delightful terraces of the great city squares, where the regulars come to escape from the heat of the sun and while away the hours smoking a hookah. The Romantic travellers of the 19th century did not fail to evoke the spell that these enthralling places had over them: Gérard de Nerval in *Journey to the Orient*, Théophile Gautier in *Constantinople* and Pierre Loti in *Aziyadé* all lovingly described the exquisite cups of Turkish coffee they savoured under the shade of plane trees or "in a large room overlooking the Bosporous" (Loti).

Above
Théodore Frère,
Interior of an Oriental café
Paris, National Museum of the Arts of Africa and Oceania

Background
The bridge from Galata to Istanbul, with the Yeni Cami mosque in the background. A popular neighbourhood in this city witnessed the birth of the first coffee houses more than four centuries ago.

Right
Pierre Loti.

Coffee for the people

Before cafés became widespread, coffee was sold by itinerant street vendors, who added the new beverage to their usual trade of water and lemonade.

THE COFFEE SELLER'S EQUIPMENT
In the 16th century the lemonade sellers of Istanbul and the water bearers of Venice started to sell coffee. These vendors had a coffee-maker kept ready to serve passers-by on demand, or to supply coffee to customers in their houses. This custom soon spread to Paris, where itinerant vendors stocked up with all the utensils needed to prepare coffee. In his *Voyage in happy Arabia* (1716), Jean de La Roque (the son of Pierre) drew a portrait of Candiot, a porter of Cretan origin who limped around the streets of Paris with a stove, a coffeemaker, a water dispenser and the sugar that was so highly prized by Parisians.

Left
A vendor selling *café au lait* on the street

Above
A coffee seller, print by Engelbrecht, c. 1735. Paris, Library of the Decorative Arts.

POPULAR TRADITION
"[Henri] found himself on the Boulevard Montmartre in the early morning, [...] he took two cigars out of his pocket, lit one from the lantern of a good woman who was selling brandy and coffee to the workers, to the street urchins, to the market gardeners, to all this Parisian population that came to life before

daybreak." This was how Balzac, in his *Girl with the Golden Eyes*, evoked the poor people's coffee that was peddled on the street, in the open air, to customers who got up early or had never owned anything remotely resembling a coffee pot. These street vendors survived in some places right up to the early 20th century, when coffee became readily available to all. Until then, many had to make do with buying a cupful of a beverage that was undoubtedly mediocre, extremely sweet and mixed with milk, but it was enough to give them the energy required to face a new day.

Below
Selling coffee by the cup on the street
When coffee arrived in Europe, poor people discovered it by means of the street hawkers.

The world of the café

"*I greatly enjoyed the café frequented by my Persian friends, on account of the variety of its regulars and the freedom of speech that reigned there.*"

GÉRARD DE NERVAL, Journey to the Orient.

Left
Café in Istanbul, with a performance by a small German orchestra. Print from 1872.

Opposite
The coffee seems to be helping these 19th-century Algerians to concentrate on their game.

If governments have always been concerned about the proliferation of cafés in cities, this is because they were often the scene of murky scheming – plans for crimes, contracts of dubious legality and forbidden gambling. They were, however, also often criticised for the frivolity that they unleashed: uninhibited language, licentious behaviour or the sheer pleasure of being with friends and having fun. The café on the street corner became a place where regulars met, like a family, to discuss the latest events in the neighbourhood or village, and where old men would spin their yarns to anybody who would listen. A whole café culture has emerged: the wrongs of the world are

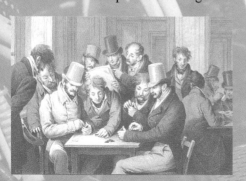

"*Four old sea dogs were sitting at the table. Two of them were playing cards and the two others watched them play: all their skin was tanned by the sun and as brown as an old oak; their hair was unkempt and greying. They looked strong and larger than life. They were emptying their cups of coffees in little sips.*"

JORIS-KARL HUYSMANS, The Dish of spices.

Above
The café, by
Edmond Morin,
c. 1860–1880.

Villanelle

Into the vintage china cup
The burning Moka pour,
Perfume of delight to sup!

Oh coffee, when you stir me up,
I see the world at war,
Within the vintage china cup.

Thanks to you, my verse rears up
And gleams like sea on shore.
Perfume of delight to sup!

It leaps about like playful pup,
And finds a rhythm raw
Within the vintage china cup.

The vapid will not fill us up;
Coffee is gallant and sure,
Perfume of delight to sup!

Black gold to which the smiths
look up;
With trembling hands they pour
Into the vintage china cup
Perfume of delight to sup!

After CHARLES MONSELET

flirt and kiss discreetly at the back of the room, while others make sure that they are seen on the more fashionable terraces. Cafés can provide a space for philosophical talks, political speeches, poetry readings, cabaret sketches or musical performances – and, in the age of the Internet café, it has become a place for chatting with somebody from the other side of the world.

righted on winter nights, while summer evenings see dancing on the terraces; whole nights are given over to dominoes, chess or cards, often played with fierce passion, and with large sums at stake; couples

"This café was above all the meeting place for certain Italian and Maltese merchant seamen, suspected of theft and smuggling."

PIERRE LOTI, Aziyadé.

Top left
The terrace of the Royal Saint-Germain, Paris.

Bottom left
Coffee waiter in La Rotonde, Paris, 1846.

Famous cafés

Following the example of the Middle East, Europe fell under the spell of these havens, where customers could enjoy a quiet coffee or meet up with friends. Most of the pioneering cafés have now disappeared, but some have proved exceptionally long-lived.

VENICE AND ROME

It is common knowledge that Italy was quick to succumb to the delights of coffee. As can be imagined, it was during the time of the Serenissima, in the 17th century, that the first cafés opened. Often little more than one dimly-lit, low-ceilinged room, they aroused great suspicion.

Women never visited them and men from high society also gave them a wide berth. It was not until the following centuries that Venetian cafés began to attract nobles, who flocked to them to play games, make commercial transactions and, above all, keep up with the latest gossip. In 1750, the dramatist Carlo Goldoni even made a Venetian café the protagonist of his play *La Bottega del Caffè*: from this ideal vantage point, he was able to conduct a witty and pitiless examination of the entire spectrum of Venetian society. Before Goldoni, however, the opening of Florian – named after its founder, Floriano Francesconi – on Saint Mark's Square in 1720 had caused a revolution: here, men and women mingled to exchange tittle-tattle and discuss current affairs. For centuries

Background
Michele Marieschi, *The Doges' Palace in Venice*. 18th century. Berlin, Charlottenburg Castle.

Right
When Saint Mark's Square in Venice is flooded, customers are served coffee in their boats!

Left
The Procope, which opened in 1686, had its finest hours in the 18th century, when several philosophers held court there. It is currently the longest-standing café in Paris.

Below
The Procope in the 18th century. Print by Badoureau, after Kretz.

all the major creative figures of Europe seemed to pass through Florian – from Musset to George Sand, from Goethe to Dickens, from Proust to Stravinsky – while locals have never ceased to meet there to learn the latest news. For Florian still exists today, in its niche under the arches of the square; lovingly restored, it now attracts tourists from all over the world. Rome had to wait until 1760 for an equivalent: the Greco, founded by a Greek of Levantine origin. Highly popular with the Romantics who visited Italy in the 19th century – Chateaubriand, Byron, Liszt and Stendhal – today the Greco is an institution that resembles a museum more than a café, as it has accumulated a motley collection of souvenirs.

Right
La Rotonde café, in the Palais-Royal, in Paris, in 1856.

Opposite
The terrace of the famous Café de la Paix, close to the Paris Opera House.

PARISIAN CAFÉS

Marseilles was not only the first French port to import coffee but was also the first to boast a café, founded in 1670 close to the Stock Exchange by an Armenian called Pascal. The business did not meet with great success, however, and its owner decided to shut up shop and try his luck further afield. If he is still remembered today, it is because he went on to be the proud owner of the very first café in Paris, which opened its doors two years later in the Foire Saint-Germain. Pride of place in the history of Parisian cafés goes, however, to a Sicilian, Procopio dei Coltelli, who opened the Procope in 1686, in premises close to the Comédie Française. It soon became the haunt of actors, but really came into its own in the period of Enlightenment, when philosophers assembled there to lay the foundations for the Revolution. Later on, the Romantics and the Symbolist poets also made it their headquarters.

THE PALAIS-ROYAL AND THE GREAT BOULEVARDS

Under Louis XV, many cafés were set up under the arches of the Palais-Royal: the Café de Foy, where Camille Desmoulins stood up one day in July 1789 to urge the crowd to revolt; the Rotonde, which forms a half-moon overlooking the palace gardens; and the Régence, founded in 1688, which witnessed memorable chess battles conducted by the young Bonaparte. In

The bars of London

Like Paris and Venice, London opened its first coffee houses at the end of the 17th century and, as elsewhere, they did not fail to provoke the hostility of prudes and politicians. London was, above all, however, the city that in the late 19th century invented "bars", where customers could drink a beer or coffee sitting on a high stool at the counter, resting their feet on a copper foot rail.

the 19th century, after major redevelopments undertaken by Haussmann, the great boulevards became the prime sites for fashionable cafés. Whole families visited them on Sunday to listen to music and watch the elegant women who strutted by.

Parisians simply cannot live without their cafés: the city already had 300 at the start of the 18th century, ten times that number in 1850 and today it has no fewer than... 15,000!

THE TURKS AND VIENNA

Austria, which invented the delicious "Viennese coffee", would perhaps not have been so fond of this drink if it had not brought them a military victory, and if coffee had not made a triumphal entrance into the country. What happened was that the Turks, determined to conquer the Balkans, were stopped in front of Vienna in 1683. They were defeated in a decisive battle and were forced to flee without delay, leaving behind

Opposite
The terrace of
the Café de
Flore in Paris in
1959. In the
heart of the
neighbourhood
of Saint-
Germain-des-
Prés, the "Flore"
has long served
as a meeting
point for writers
and artists. It is
still fashionable
today.

Left
The Central in
Vienna, in the
late 19th
century. Print by
Armand Kohl,
after Franz
Kollarz.

Below left
A water in the
Helder café,
Paris.

significant amounts of their precious coffee. A Polish war hero, General Kolschitzky, helped himself to this booty and opened the Blue Bottle, Vienna's first café. Its success gave rise to a host of imitators.

In the 19th century, all the cafés strove to attract cultural figures: Brahms was a regular in the Herrenhof, while Mahler preferred the Imperial. Later on, the Sacher café invented the chocolate cake that provides such a perfect accompaniment to coffee, and Trotsky used to play chess in the Central café. The Viennese have turned the café into an institution which they visit in the mornings to read a newspaper – the custom of making the daily papers available to customers has remained intact to this day -— and return to in the afternoon to enjoy a pastry, or at weekends to listen to classical music.

A coffee and croissant

To celebrate the Austrian victory over the Ottoman army in 1683, the cake makers of Venice had the idea of inventing a new pastry, which they deridingly gave the form of a symbol of Islam: the crescent moon. So it is that for over three centuries a military triumph has been celebrated in cafés by hastily downing... a coffee and croissant!

One and a half
billion cups

One and a half billion: that is the number of cups of coffee drunk every day on the planet! The coffee service has long ceased to be reserved for ceremonial occasions. Although changes in design trends and lifestyles have led to a greater emphasis on simplicity, the pleasure of gathering round a table is as potent as ever and plenty of occasions still present themselves to enjoy a good cup of coffee with family or friends.

Eastern rituals

Whether coffee is served to guests in a tent – in the style of the nomads of the Sahara or the Bedouins of Arabia – or in the intimacy of a home, it is accompanied by traditions that are still flourishing today.

DESERT CEREMONIES

Since time immemorial, the nomads of the Sahara have prepared coffee in front of their tent, in full view of their guests: after roasting and crushing the beans, the powder is mixed with water and boiled successively in three coffee pots of different size. The grounds are then allowed to sink to the bottom before serving. In order to obtain good results, the ceremony must take its time and scrupulously follow the different stages: when everything is finally ready, the person responsible for the brew tastes it before pouring it into the awaiting row of small glasses. Although these preparations have been somewhat simplified in recent times, several coffee pots are still used, and the ritual is always performed in front of guests.

Above
A pause by the tent while crossing the Atlas Mountains.

Morocco, 1910–1914.
Bottom left
Woman pouring coffee for guests in Ethiopia.

TURKISH COFFEE

Coffee in Turkey was traditionally made by slaves, and the women in a harem had servants whose sole function was to prepare this drink. Before being served it was decanted into a metal jug – or a gold one in the Court – called an *ibrik*. The sultans of Istanbul were also the first to own what we would now call "coffee services", consisting of an *ibrik* with a long spout and some tiny china cups. Porcelain had been brought back from China by Marco Polo in the 13th century, and it had immediately won favour with the Ottoman rulers. The small cups they used were egg-shaped, with no handles, and they rested on supports called *zarf*. In *Aziyadé* Pierre Loti described how "Aziyadé was brought his Turkish coffee in the accustomed manner, in a blue cup about as big as half an egg, set on a copper base". This coffee was generally accompanied by a glass of water, "which the Turks drink before and the French afterwards", as Théophile Gautier verified, following a custom that still exists in the Eastern Mediterranean.

Above
Servant presenting coffee, Algeria.

Left
A café in Algeria.

Elegance at the table

Europe discovered three exotic drinks at almost the same time: tea, coffee and chocolate, and these soon became a part of everyday life.
It was not until the 18th century, however, that specific objects appeared to serve these new delicacies.

OBJECTS FOR SERVING COFFEE

The arrival of coffee on European tables drastically changed the customs surrounding it: just as serving dishes had been created to avoid placing saucepans in front of guests, so refined and elegant pots had to be invented to serve coffee. At first there was little distinction between pots for tea, coffee and chocolate. For a long time, the pear-shape Arabic coffee pot provided the only reference, and its spout and handle inspired designs for all three drinks. Eventually, however, artists started looking for alternatives, and European coffee pots began to reflect the latest fashions.

THE CRAZE FOR PORCELAIN

The arrival of tea and coffee in Europe led to the discovery of hot drinks (until then only wine and other cold beverages had been known). Metal goblets proved unsuitable for hot liquids and soon gave way to porcelain from China. This remained expensive, however, as the Chinese jealously guarded the secrets of how to manufacture porcelain. Less wealthy households would not have access to porcelain until the emergence of the first major manufacturers in Europe. This was when technical expertise joined forces with imagination to create original motifs to decorate coffee pots.

Above
Arabic-style coffee pot made by Christofle.

Above
Tasting tea, coffee and chocolate, detail from Delftware,
c. 1710. Sèvres, National Pottery Museum.

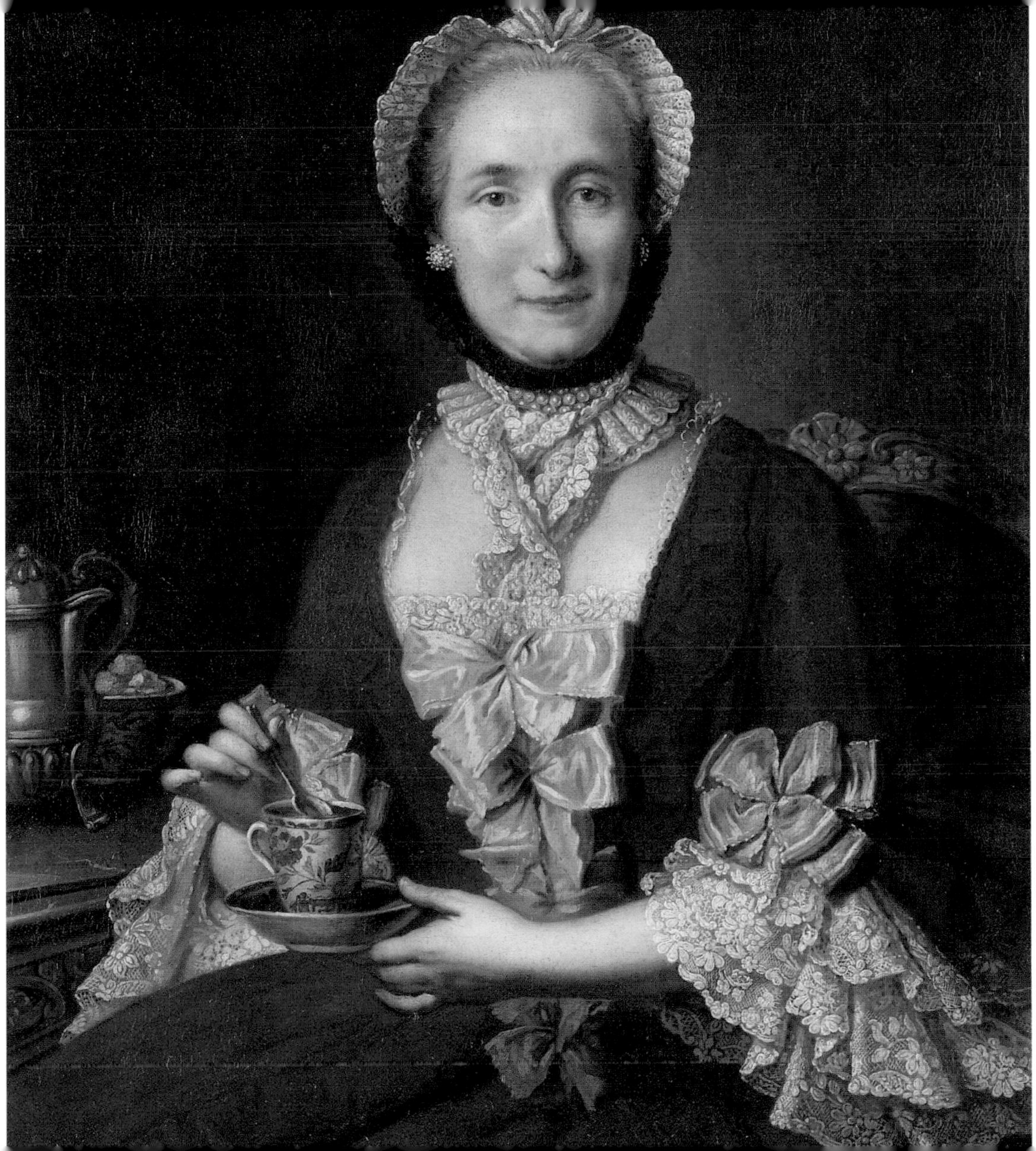

Left
Christofle coffee pots in silver plate ornamented with guilloche. On the right, the Pine Cone model, 1900.

Below
Contemporary

service: Bagatelle, by Christofle.

Previous page
Woman holding a cup of coffee. 18th-century French school. Roubaix, Museum of Art and Industry.

LUXURY ON THE TABLE

Aristocrats love anything that glimmers and, from the late 17th century, their wishes were granted with copper or silver coffee pots. Two centuries later, the bourgeoisie also began to covet sophisticated coffee services.

The development of silver plating techniques enabled them to satisfy their whims; solid silver was gradually displaced by silver plate, which made it possible to create finely wrought coffee services inspired by the workmanship of traditional

Left
A service for tea or coffee,

1925, Christofle

silversmiths. In the 1840s one such silversmith, Christofle, perfected an electrochemical technique involving the superimposition of silver particles onto objects made from nickel silver (an alloy of nickel, copper and zinc). He produced some models of coffee pots in this way and met with immediate success. Such works of art were, however, also complemented by pieces that were more everyday and functional, but equally elegant.

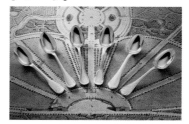

An example of original design: in this service, the three elements – coffee pot, milk jug and sugar bowl – are stacked on top of each other. Christofle, Fjerdingstad, c. 1925.

ENAMEL IN KITCHENS

A world away from Sèvres china and exclusive silversmiths, coffee pots also found their way into more humble kitchens. The first models were made of earthenware, with a filter, but as soon as enamelled iron appeared in the late 19th century this became the material of choice. Pots appeared in all sizes, in a motley range of colours and decorations – flowers, animals or stencilled geometrical motifs. These cheap and cheerful coffee pots, mass-produced in Holland, Belgium and northern France, had pride of place on our grandparents' tables, and even today they find eager buyers in flea markets.

Left
Coffee pot from the 1930s, Aubecq factory. Auxile-Château Museum.

The coffee service

The coffee service, which first appeared around 1700, comprises a pot, a sugar bowl, a milk jug and a number of cups, ranging from one or two to six. This classic format is still highly prized today, but has gradually modernised and sometimes takes on unexpected shapes and colours – although the survival of the tradition encourages companies to create timeless models, to the detriment of more adventurous interpretations.

Enthusiasts all over the world

*Who drinks coffee today?
The British drink 165
million cups a day, but
suppliers are still trying to
diversify the market and win
over young people by means
of special offers and new
flavours.*

EACH TO THEIR OWN

What is best for drinking
coffee: a big mug, a small
porcelain cup, a rustic bowl?
It does not really matter, as all
coffee drinkers have their
own preferences, shaped by
regional customs. Coffee cups
have their history too.

The first came from
China, but they were bell-
shape dishes more suited to
tea. When the two beverages
finally established their own
distinct identities, cups also
came into their own, with
large, open
ones for tea and taller, narrower ones for coffee.
Handles first appeared in the 18th century, at
almost the same time as the saucer. It was not unusual to
pour a little coffee in the saucer to allow it to cool, and
the custom of drinking coffee sip by sip from the saucer
lasted until the early 20th century in Europe, and persists
today in Asian countries like Indonesia.

Modern coffee cups have emphasised the visual aspect;
whether made of stark white china or decorated with
coloured motifs, they reflect the tastes of the period. Coffee
served in bars and restaurants – especially Espresso – requires
thicker cups (so that the liquid stays hot until it reaches the table)
and a slight bell shape (so that the foam stays in a uniform layer).

Below
Coffee pot from
the Follement
series, made by
Christian Lacroix
Arts de la Table.

Above
Messidor coffee
service from
Christofle.

DISPELLING THE MYTHS

No survey of the world of coffee would be complete without a brief comparison of the amounts of coffee that Italy is one of the greatest consumers of coffee in the world but, as so often, the statistics reveal otherwise.

Below
Coffee cup from the Floral breakfast service, by Christofle.

Bottom
Coffee in the garden of a French family, in 1910.

The Espresso cups marketed by Illy have become collectors' items. Here, the Schwung series by Peter Roesch.

Northern Europeans are the greatest coffee consumers of all: 11.6 kg per inhabitant per year in Finland, closely followed by the Scandinavian countries (Sweden, Denmark and Norway). This hot drink has obviously found a hearty welcome in inhospitable climates. Austria, Holland, Switzerland and Germany form the next group (with a consumption of 8 to 10 kg per inhabitant per year), with France coming next in 9th place, on 5.9 kg per year, way ahead of the Mediterranean countries. Italy straggles in with a mere 4.4 kg per year, just behind the United States – but even that is twice the consumption of the British!

Opposite
Coffee has undoubtedly gained in quality, but it no longer stands on ceremony. Here, coffee is served after a meal, in the 1950s.

Coffee and young people

Coffee merchants have to confront the fact that their customers are not in the spring of life: their product fails to attract young people, who prefer soft drinks and are repelled by the bitterness of coffee. Nevertheless, to help young people discover coffee, some companies have tried complementing traditional beverages like cappuccino with flavoured coffees. Undeterred by the outrage of purists, they have launched coffees flavoured with vanilla, orange, lemon and even mint. The stir created by these novelties has attracted a public, albeit confined to the West Coast of the United States and a few trendy cafés in some European cities. Elsewhere, they have been a huge flop; anybody who really wants to introduce young people to the delights of coffee will just have to wait until they are a little bit older!

A few recipes…

Originally confined to its role as a hot drink, coffee has gradually seeped into all types of dishes, first as a choice ingredient for desserts – especially when mixed with cream – before entering more recently into the domain of alcoholic cocktails and savoury sauces.

A few coffee recipes

SAVOURY DISHES

Roast fillets of duck and braised chicory, in a sauce with infusion of Arabica

Recipe supplied by Jean-Michel Lorain (restaurant La Côte Saint-Jacques, Joigny)

Serves 4
4 fillets of duck
2 cups (500 ml) duck stock
2 oz/40 g butter
4 chicories
4 lemons
2 oz/40 g Arabica beans
1 sprig flat-leaved parsley
salt, sugar, pepper

• Preparation:

Cut the lemon peel into strips and cook them in a light syrup made up of water and sugar.

Steam the chicories over a low heat, then dry them off in a colander.

Sauté the fillets of duck, without allowing them to lose their pink colour. Take them out of the pan and put them aside on a plate.

Deglaze the same pan with a ladleful of water, add the duck stock and heat, reducing the sauce by half.

Crush the coffee beans and add them to the sauce, bring it to the boil and allow it to infuse for 10 minutes.

Add the butter to the sauce and adjust the seasoning to taste.

Cut the chicories lengthwise into two and fry them in butter, adding salt, pepper and sugar to taste until they are slightly caramelised.

Heat the duck fillets in the frying pan.

• Presentation:

Using 4 flat plates, arrange two endive halves in a fan shape on the upper part of each plate.

Put one duck fillet, divided into three pieces, onto each plate.

Add one spoonful of lemon peel and cover the bottom of the plates with sauce. Decorate each plate with a flat parsley leaf.

Matelote of salmon with coffee, fricassee of kidney beans and pickling onions

Recipe supplied by Yasuo Nanaumi (restaurant of the Maison de l'Amérique Latine, Paris)

Serves 6
2 lb/900 g salmon fillets without skin or bones
2 cups/500 ml red wine
4 oz/80 g butter
5 cups cold, fairly strong Espresso coffee
3 shallots
1 sprig flat-leaved parsley
1 leek
1 teaspoon of potato flour

For the garnish:
8 oz/250 g dried kidney beans
12 new pickling onions with their green stalks
6 Paris mushrooms
6 shiitake onions
4 oz/80 g butter
1 bouquet garni
1 onion
Half a carrot
salt, pepper, sugar

• Preparation:

Soak the kidney beans overnight in cold water, then drain.

In a pressure cooker, cook the beans, the onion cut in half, the bouquet garni and the carrot for 30 min in two volumes of water. Add seasoning. Put aside.

Brown all the mushrooms in half the butter. Put aside.

Glaze the pickling onions in a saucepan over a low heat, with a little water, the rest of the butter and 1 teaspoon of sugar. Put aside.

Cut the fillets lengthwise into two, then cut each half into three equal parts. Roll them up, tying them in place with string.

Mix the red wine, chopped shallots, coffee, parsley and slivered leek in a saucepan.

Bring to the boil and add the fillets of salmon. Cover and cook over a low heat for 10 to 15 min.

Mix the kidney beans, onions and mushrooms. Adjust the seasoning to taste and keep simmering.

Take out the salmon fillets and reduce the sauce by half, adding 1 teaspoonful of potato flour thinned in a little red wine. Add the butter in knobs, stirring vigorously. Add seasoning.

• Presentation:

Place the garnish on the plates. Add the fillets of salmon and pour the sauce around them.

Fillets of mackerel marinated in coffee with turnip vinaigrette

Recipe supplied by Yasuo Nanaumi (restaurant of the Maison de l'Amérique Latine, Paris)

Serves 6

3 small mackerels (filleted)
12 potatoes (Ratte)
12 oz/350 g long turnips
Fine Guérande salt
Half a teaspoon vanilla sugar
Half a teaspoon ground pepper
1 tbsp/12 g ground coffee
3 tablespoons white vinegar
1 tablespoon sherry vinegar
1 tablespoon soy sauce
4 tablespoons olive oil
Herbs (chervil, chives, flat-leaved parsley)

• Preparation:

Spread the mackerel fillets in a flat dish, with the skin facing upwards. Mix 20 g of salt, the sugar and the pepper, and sprinkle this mixture over the fillets.

Cover the fillets with ground coffee and leave to marinate overnight.

The next day, remove the salt and coffee by lightly tapping the fillets.

Pour the white vinegar into a shallow dish and soak the fillets, skin side down, for 3 min. Remove the skin from the fillets.

Prepare the vinaigrette: grate a turnip of around 2 oz/50 g and put it in a salad bowl. Add salt, sherry vinegar and soy sauce. Mix well, adding olive oil all the while. Put aside.

Prepare the garnish: peel, clean and coarsely grate the rest of the turnips. Refresh them in cold water, changing the water several times. Strain and season with 2 tablespoons of vinaigrette and chopped herbs. Put aside.

Boil the potatoes in their skin in salted water, then drain.

Cut the mackerel fillets into thin slices.

• Presentation:

Put two, warm, unpeeled potatoes, cut into halves, onto each plate.

Spread the slices of mackerel in layers over the potatoes.

Add the grated turnips and sprinkle the fillets with vinaigrette.

Coffee éclairs

For 6 éclairs
For the choux pastry:
4 eggs
5 oz/125 g flour
3 oz/80 g butter
1 tbsp/15 g sugar
1 cup/250 ml water
1 pinch salt

For the coffee cream:
1 whole egg + 1 yolk
2 cups/500 ml milk
5 tbsps/40 g flour

3 oz/75 g sugar
2 tablespoons coffee extract

• Preparation:

Start with the cream: boil the milk in a pan with the coffee extract.

Mix the flour, eggs and sugar in a bowl.

Add the milk little by little, return the mixture to the pan, and simmer over a very low heat, stirring constantly. Do not allow to boil. Remove from heat and leave to cool.

For the choux pastry: put the water, butter, salt and sugar into a saucepan. Heat to boiling point, remove from the heat, pour the flour into the mixture in one go and stir vigorously.

Put the dough mixture back onto a low heat until it forms a homogenous ball that can easily be detached from the sides of the saucepan.

Remove from the heat and add the whole eggs, one by one, stirring constantly. Leave to cool.

Spread small sausages of choux pastry, around 6 in long, on a pastry tray covered with greaseproof paper, spacing them out so that they will not touch when risen. Bake in a hot oven for about 20 min, remove, and leave to cool.

Gently make an incision down one side of each and fill with the cream, using an icing bag. Decorate with ready-made coffee fondant.

Walnut cake with coffee and chocolate sauce

Serves 6
4 egg yolks
6 oz/150 g sugar
1 tablespoon cornflour
1 tbsp/15 g butter
1 glass milk
1 scant cup/200 ml cream
12 oz/300 g shelled walnuts
12 oz/300 g plain chocolate
1 tablespoon bitter cocoa powder
1 cup strong coffee

• Preparation:

Chop the walnuts in a blender, reserving a few for decoration.

Beat the egg yolks and the sugar until the mixture turns white and then add the cornflour.

Melt 4 oz/100 g of chocolate with

the milk in a saucepan and pour into the egg mixture, stirring vigorously to obtain a homogenous dough. Add the chopped walnuts and mix them in.

Pour the mixture into a mould greased with butter and bake in a preheated oven at a medium temperature (150° C, gas mark 2) for 25 min.

When the cake has cooled, take it out of the mould and sprinkle the top with the cocoa powder. Decorate with the reserved walnuts.

Just before serving, prepare the sauce: melt the remaining 200 g of chocolate with the coffee in a saucepan. Remove from the heat and add the cream, stirring well. Serve the sauce while it is still warm, beside the cake.

Coffee soufflé

Serves 6
4oz/100 g butter
2 oz/50 g flour
5 oz/125 g sugar
2 cups/500 ml milk
5 eggs
2 teaspoons coffee extract

• Preparation:
Boil the milk with the sugar and the coffee extract.

In another saucepan, prepare a béchamel sauce with the butter, flour and milk mixture.

Add the egg yolks one by one, stirring each time. Leave to cool.

Whisk the egg whites until they are stiff and gently fold them into the mixture.

Butter a soufflé dish and put into the oven at a medium temperature (160° C, gas mark 2) for about 30 min. Serve immediately.

Tiramisu

Serves 6
2 whole eggs + 2 yolks
1lb/500 g mascarpone
4 oz/100 g sugar
2 scant cups/400 ml very strong decaffeinated coffee
1 scant cup/200 ml dry red vermouth
40 sponge fingers
Unsweetened cocoa powder

• Preparation of the cream:
Beat the egg yolks and sugar thoroughly. Add the mascarpone.

Mix carefully by hand and add 2 stiffly beaten egg whites.

• Preparation of the coffee:
Mix two parts of coffee and one part of vermouth, ensuring the mixture is bitter.

• Presentation:
Cover the bottom of a 3 in high, flat-bottomed dish with a tightly packed layer of biscuits, soaking them in the coffee mixture.

Add a layer of the mascarpone cream and continue alternating layers, finishing with biscuits.

Leave in the refrigerator for at least 6 hours.

Before serving, sprinkle a thin layer of unsweetened cocoa powder onto the tiramisu.

NB: Tiramisu can be frozen without any problem, but it must be allowed to thaw gently for 12 hr before serving.

Tulips with coffee mousse

Serves 6
For the tulips:
3 egg yolks
5 oz/125 g flaked almonds
Scant 2 oz/40 g butter
2 tbsps/15 g flour
3 oz/75 g sugar

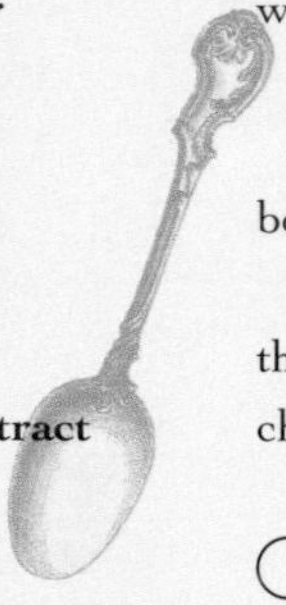

For the mousse:
4 egg whites
3 oz/75 g sugar
2 teaspoons coffee extract

• Preparation:

Prepare the mousse first: whisk the egg whites until stiff. Add the sugar and continue whisking, while adding the coffee extract. Leave in the refrigerator for 2 hours.

Prepare the tulips: mix the flour, sugar and egg yolks in a salad bowl. Add the melted butter, then the almonds. Leave to rest for 1_ hrs in a cool place.

Preheat the oven to 150° C (gas mark 2). Put 3 tablespoons of the tulip dough on a sheet of greaseproof paper and flatten them out into very thin disks about 5 inches in diameter. Bake for about 8 min

Remove the tulips with a spatula. While they are still warm, put each one into a bowl, making sure that the tulip takes on its form. Prepare the second half of the dough in the same way.

• Presentation:

Gently ease the tulips out of the bowls and put them on a plate.

Just before serving, fill them with the coffee mousse and decorate with chocolate-coated coffee beans.

DRINKS

Viennese coffee

Prepare a fairly weak Espresso – if possible from a somewhat light-roasted coffee. Add hot milk beaten with whipped cream and sprinkle with chocolate powder.

Cappuccino

Contrary to popular belief, the authentic Italian cappuccino does not contain whipped cream.

Prepare an Espresso in a large cup, without filling it completely. Add a little milk heated with steam in the machine, in order to obtain a very creamy mousse. Sprinkle with a little bitter cocoa.

Irish Coffee

This alcoholic drink is prepared in a large glass with a stem, using one part of whisky for three parts of coffee. Add sugar, stir and pour a few spoonfuls of chilled whipped cream on to the surface of the liquid.

Iced coffee

This highly refreshing summer drink was invented in Italy but has gone on to find favour in many hot countries.

Prepare a strong Espresso and leave it to cool. Put some ice cups in a glass, add the cold coffee and, if so desired, a little milk and sugar.

Bibliography

HISTORICAL WORKS ON COFFEE

Avicenne, *Canon de la médecine* (11th century).
Prosper Alpini, *Plantes d'Égypte* (1580).
Honoré de Balzac, *Traité des excitants modernes* (1833).
Nicolas de Blégny, *Le Bon Usage du thé, du café et du chocolat* (1687).
Brillat-Savarin, *Physiologie du goût*
Philippe Sylvestre Dufour, *Traité nouveau et curieux du café* (1684).
Jean de La Roque, *Voyage de l'Arabie heureuse* (1716).
Jean-Baptiste Tavernier, *Les Six Voyages de J-B Tavernier* (1676).
Alexis Cadet de Vaux, *Dissertation sur le café* (1806).

LITERATURE AND COFFEE

Blixen Karen, *Out of Africa*.
Colette, *La Maison de Claudine*.
Flaubert Gustave, *Notes du voyage en Orient*.
Goldoni Carlo, *La Bottega del Caffè*.
Loti Pierre, *Aziyadé*.
Montesquieu, *Les Lettres persanes*.
de Nerval Gérard, *Le Voyage en Orient*.
de Saint-Pierre Bernardin, *Paul et Virginie*.
Voltaire, *Candide*.

MODERN WORKS ON COFFEE OR COFFEE-RELATED ITEMS

Alessi Alberto, *L'Usine à rêves*, Electa/Alessi, 1998.
Boe, Philippe, *Coffee*, Cassell & Co, 2001.
Bramah Edward, *Coffeepots and coffee makers*, PML Éditions, 1991.
Dicum, Gregory, *The Coffee Book*, The New Press, 1999.
Ellis, Hattie, *Coffee: Discovering, Exploring*, Ryland, Peters & Small, 2002.
Hardy Christophe, *Le café, des mots et des saveurs*, Herscher, 1998.
Heise Ulla, *Histoire du café et des cafés les plus célèbres*, Belfond, Paris, 1988 pour la traduction française.
Illy Francesco et Riccardo, *Du café à l'express*, Abbeville, 1992.
Jobin Philippe et Van Leckwyck Bernard, *Coffee*, Nathan, 1988.
Massia Pierre, Rombouts Hugo et Blanc Jean-Pierre, *La Passion du café par Malongo*, Artis Historia, Bruxelles, 1995.
Mauro Frédéric, *Histoire du café*, Desjonquères, Paris, 1991.
Reekie, Jennie, *The Little Coffee Book*, Piatkus, 1985.
Rolnick Harry, *The Complete Book of Coffee*, Rolf Stacker, 1982.
Stella Alain, *Abécédaire du café*, Flammarion, Paris, 1998.
Uribe, Andres C, *Brown Gold: The Amazing Story of Coffee*, Random House, 1955.

and… a few website addresses:
www.coffeeuniverse.com
www.ineedcoffee.com
www.arabica.org
www.coffeeresearch.org
www.coffeescience.org
www.ico.org

Previous page
Almond, *Still life with coffee pot*.
Paris, Orsay Museum.

Some addresses

• **Association of Coffee Producing Countries**
5th Floor, Suite B
7/10 Old Park Lane
London W1Y 3LJ

• **International Coffee Association**
22 Berners Street
London W1P 4DD

• **National Coffee Association of USA**
15 Maiden Lane, Suite 1405
New York, NY 10038-4003

• **Specialty Coffee Association of America/Specialty Coffee Institute**
1 World Trade Center, Suite 1200
Long Beach, CA 90831-1200

• **Musée Jacobs Suchard**
Seefelquai, 17
8034 Zurich (Suisse)

A SELECTION OF LONDON CAFÉS

• **Bar Italia (est. 1949)**
22 Frith Street
Soho
London W1V 5TS

• **Café Valerie (original tea house opened 1725)**
8 Russell Street
Covent Garden
London WC2 5HZ

• **Caffé Carluccio's**
12 West Smithfield
London EC1A 9JR

• **Caffé Carluccio's**
8 Market Place
Fitzrovia
London W1W 8AG

• **Konditor & Cook**
66 The Cut
London SE1 8LZ

• **Pâtisserie Valerie (est 1926)**
44 Old Compton Street
Soho
London W1D 5JX

• **Pâtisserie Valerie (previously Sagne's, est 1921)**
105 Marylebone High Street
London W1U 4RS

• **Raison d'Étre**
18 Bute Street
London SW7 3EX

'The King of Coffee, by Aubé', Rue de l'Isly, No. 17. *Coffee is acclaimed by true connoisseurs as the strongest and most exquisite of all the beverages that have appeared to date. When it is burnt by means of a new process, it acquires a superior taste and strength.*

Acknowledgements

The author extends sincere thanks
to all those who helped make this book possible,
especially:

Madame Catherine Cotelle, Association de Clieu •
Madame Geneviève Jobin • Jean-Pierre Blanc, Chairman, cafés Malongo •
Emmanuel Despierres, Chairman, Comité Français du Café •
Éric Duchossy, cafés Verlet • Pierre Massia, teacher •
Jean-Jacques Perriot, researcher, CIRAD

Not forgetting:
Pascal Achard (Centre Culturel de la Castine) •
Jacques-Lionel Aubert (W.A.) • Josée Deteuf (cafés Malongo) •
Séverine Fasquelle (Lavazza, France) • Laurent Fougères (Comptoirs Coffea) •
Benoît Grison (Segafredo-Zanetti,) • Anne Gros (musée Christofle) •
Sylvie Laurent (La Maison du Café) • Patrick Masson et Ludovic Maillard
(Maison Jobin) • Monsieur Meauxsonne (cafés Méo) •
Christine Pascolo (Illycaffè, Trieste) • Ennio Ranaboldo et Marcello Arcangeli
(Lavazza, Turin) • Christine Rault (Comité Français du Café) •
Nathalie Roland (K.J.S.) • Florence Rossilion (SNICC) •
Pierre Schulé (cafés Sati) • Thierry Verpillon (Illy, France)
Les cafés Legal, Négrita, Richard, Nestlé-France,
Alessi, Bodum, Christian Lacroix Arts de la Table, Christofle, Moulinex,
La Société des Philatélistes, Lucrezia Bufano, Catherine Sauvat,
Jean-Michel Lorain (restaurant La Côte Saint-Jacques, Joigny),
Catherine Prain-Salles et Nanaumi Yasuo
(Maison de l'Amérique Latine, à Paris)

Photographic credits

Editors : Cécile AOUSTIN et Valérie TOGNALI
Designer : Sabine HOUPLAIN
Layout: Nadine GAUTIER-QUENTIN